Willing Slaves of Capital

Spinoza and Marx on Desire

Frédéric Lordon

Translated by Gabriel Ash

CW00544861

VERSO

London • New York

First published by Verso 2014
Translation © Gabriel Ash 2014
Originally published as *Capitalisme, désir et servitude*
© La fabrique éditions 2010

3 5 7 9 10 8 6 4

Verso
UK: 6 Meard Street, London W1F 0EG
US: 20 Jay Street, Suite 1010, Brooklyn, NY 11201
www.versobooks.com

Verso is the imprint of New Left Books

ISBN-13: 978-1-78168-160-2 (PBK)
ISBN-13: 978-1-78168-161-9 (HBK)
eISBN-13: 978-1-78168-213-5 (US)
eISBN-13: 978-1-78168-635-5 (UK)

British Library Cataloguing in Publication Data
A catalogue record for this book is available from the British Library.

Library of Congress Cataloging-in-Publication Data
A catalog record for this book is available from the Library of Congress.

Typeset in Minion Pro by Hewer Text UK Ltd, Edinburgh
Printed and bound by CPI Group (UK) Ltd, Croydon, CR0 4YY

Contents

WALLACE: Not only that, Mr Fage. You have to understand the business, so that your ideas go in a specific direction . . . the relationship between the company and the new employee must be a little bit like a marriage of love.

Michel Vinaver, *The Job Application*

We are taught that businesses have souls, which is surely the most terrifying news in the world.

Gilles Deleuze, 'Postscript on the Societies of Control'

Were it as easy to control people's minds as to restrain their tongues, every sovereign would rule securely and there would be no oppressive governments. For all men would live according to the minds of those who govern them and would judge what is true or false, or good or bad, in accordance with their decree alone. But . . . it is impossible for one person's mind to be absolutely under another's control. For no one can transfer to another person his natural right, or ability, to think freely and make his own judgments about any matter whatsoever, and cannot be compelled to do so. This is why a government which seeks to control people's minds is considered oppressive . . .

Spinoza, *Theological-Political Treatise*

Foreword

Capitalism keeps making itself contentious. Were it not at times such a repulsive spectacle, one could almost admire the audacity with which it tramples the main tenet of the very body of thought that it flaunts as its ideological reference; for it is indeed liberalism that commands, here in Kant's formulation, to 'act in such a way that you treat humanity, whether in your own person or in the person of any other, always at the same time as an end and never simply as a means'.[1] Yet, in a dialectical reversal peculiar to major advances in social control, the idea that some are free to use others as means to an end, while others are free to allow themselves to be used in that manner, has been proclaimed the very essence of freedom. The superb meeting point of these two freedoms is called employment [*salariat*].[2]

Étienne de La Boétie reminds us how the habit of serving leads to losing sight of the very condition of servitude.[3] It is not that people 'forget' the unhappiness caused by servitude; but they endure its misfortunes as a *destiny* over which they have no choice, or even simply as a way of life to which one eventually becomes accustomed. Successful enslavements break the connection

---

1   Immanuel Kant, *Grounding of Metaphysics of Morals*, 3rd ed., trans. James W. Ellington, Hackett, 1993, p. 36 (4:429).

2   In French, *salariat* and *patronat* denote both the condition or institution of respectively being employed and owning a business, and the classes of people involved – the workforce and the owners of businesses respectively. Depending on context, the various derivations of 'employ' are used in the first case (employment, employee, and employee-class, and wage-labour and workforce when more appropriate). Because the usage of *patronat* is idiosyncratic, it and its cognates are translated by comparable derivations of the English word 'boss'. [Trans.]

3   Étienne de La Boétie, *The Discourse of Voluntary Servitude*, Hackett, 2012.

between the sad affects of enslavement and the consciousness of being enslaved. For it is the clarity of the latter realisation that always risks rekindling thoughts of revolt. La Boétie's warning must be kept in mind if we are to return to the 'hard core' of capitalist servitude to square the depth of its incrustation with how little amazement it elicits. But amazing it is: a few – we call them bosses – have the 'power'[4] to convince the many to adopt their employers' desires as if they were their own and to occupy themselves in their service.

Does this 'power' – a very strange one, upon reflection – really belong to them? Thanks to Marx we are well aware that it does not. Rather, it is the effect of a particular configuration of social structures: the employment relation is the double separation of the workers from both the means of production and from its products. These structures, however, do not explain everything that takes place inside capitalist organisations, a task that belongs to the psychology and sociology of work. Rather than seeking to contribute to these distinctive disciplines, this book proposes a more abstract approach, although one which may hold some useful elements for them to draw on: to combine a structuralism of relations and an anthropology of passions – Marx and Spinoza.

These two have certainly met, if only through their commentators. While they are not in complete agreement, their affinities are legion, or in any case sufficiently strong that bringing them together would not run the risk of producing nonsense. The temporal paradox is that, although Marx comes after Spinoza, it is Spinoza who can now help us fill the gaps in Marx. For identifying the structures of the capitalist mobilisation of employees does not

---

4 The English word 'power' has two meanings that French (and Latin) distinguish with two separate words. *Puissance* (Latin *potentia*) can be thought of as inherent power (ability, power of acting, doing), whereas *pouvoir* (Latin *potestas*), as in the case above, stands for relational, differential power (power over, social power, political power, etc.). [Trans.]

tell us what these structures 'run on'; that is to say, it does not tell us what, concretely, makes them effective – not the ghost but the engine in the machine. The Spinozist answer is *affects*.

Social life is just another name for the collective passionate life. Of course, this life is organised through institutional forms that introduce considerable differences, but within which affects and forces of desire continue to be the *primum mobile*. Recognising their deeply structured character does not therefore preclude a re-examination of the employment question 'through the passions', thus asking afresh how capital's few succeed in making labour's many work for them, and according to which regimes of mobilisation. On the contrary, returning to this question may even make it possible to find the common ground between disparate facts such as the following: employees go to work to avoid starving; their enjoyment as consumers compensates them to a greater or lesser extent for their taxing toil; some spend all their waking hours working, and appear satisfied; others enthusiastically join in the running of the company; then, one day, they rebel (or throw themselves out of the window).

For contemporary capitalism undeniably displays a much richer landscape of passions, with much stronger contrasts, than it did in Marx's time. Intent on retaining the centrality of the confrontation between the two monoliths of 'capital' and 'labour', Marxism took a long time to acknowledge that fact, not without paying a certain price. Was not the credibility of the binary class scheme considerably damaged by the historical rise of the managers, those strange employees, materially on the side of labour but symbolically on the side of capital?[5] The

---

5   Marxist theory has caught up with this issue to a great extent, notably thanks to the work of Gérard Duménil and Dominique Lévy, who explicitly formulated the 'management hypothesis'. See *Économie marxiste du capitalisme*, La Découverte, 2003. See also Jacques Bidet and Gérard Duménil, *Altermarxisme. Un autre marxisme pour un autre monde*, PUF, 2007.

manager is the very model for the kind of happy workforce that
capitalism would like to create – regardless of the manifest
contradiction that simultaneously drives capitalism, in its
neoliberal configuration, to *also* regress towards the most brutal
forms of coercion. The idea of domination could not avoid
being affected by this development; approached simplistically, it
is unsettled by the spectacle of the happily dominated.

Countless works have grappled with this paradox, notably
within the sociological tradition indebted to Pierre Bourdieu,
whose concept of symbolic violence aimed precisely at thinking through the intersections of domination and consent.
Nevertheless, the (conceptual) terrain of capitalist domination remains open: how can one make sense of this concept –
setting aside the cases where employees are downright (and
actively) terrorised – when many employees appear to do
more than merely adapt to their job, find little to complain
about in it, and at times appear to derive real satisfaction from
it? But making the dominated happy so that they forget their
domination is one of the oldest and most effective ruses of the
art of ruling. Under the impact of the requirements of its new
productive forms, and helped by the growing sophistication of
its practices of governmentality, capitalism is on the road to
achieving a domination that no longer shows the familiar face
of the naked iron yoke.

Of course, the sociology of work did set out to peek behind
the gleaming façade of the idea of consent and expose its short-
comings, but without always asking what should be the very
first question: what exactly does 'consent' mean? This question
is worth asking, since by leaving the matter unresolved one
risks seeing the facts of 'consent' (where they exist) destabilise
the concepts of exploitation, alienation, and domination,
concepts that Marxist critique in particular relies upon as the
trusted foundations of its intellectual toolkit. Each of these
concepts is perturbed by the new, 'motivational' managerial

tendencies that promise 'fulfilment at work' and 'self-realisation', and that appear at times to be winning the support of employees. Testifying to that destabilising effect is the relative conceptual impoverishment that, in the absence of anything better, leads to the persistent reappearance of that trite expression, 'voluntary servitude'. While it is no doubt a suggestive oxymoron, its flaws – those owing to the very fact that it is an oxymoron – come to light as soon as it passes from poetry into theory (setting aside the eponymous work).

To feel mobilised, or vaguely reluctant, or even rebellious, to commit one's labour-power enthusiastically or grudgingly, are so many different ways of being affected as an employee, that is, of being made [*déterminé*] to join in the realisation of a plan (a desire) that was not initially one's own. This is then, perhaps, the elementary triangle inside which the mystery of being recruited in another person's service (in its capitalist form) should be resituated: one person's desire, others' power of acting, and the affects – produced by the structures of the employment relation that determine their encounter. It is here, at the intersection of the Spinozist anthropology of passions and the Marxist theory of wage-labour, that it becomes possible to rethink the concepts of exploitation and alienation from the ground up, and thus ultimately to reopen the discussion about capitalism (but always in the two senses of criticism and analysis). And with that comes also the hope that capitalism can at last move from being merely contentious to being transcended.

CHAPTER ONE

Making Others Do Something

THE DESIRE TO DO SOMETHING

Spinoza calls conatus the effort by which 'each thing, as far as it can by its own power, strives to persevere in its being.'[1] This phrase takes a certain effort to decipher, and those discovering it for the first time struggle to understand what is meant by this perseverance in being, what kind of concrete action it designates or makes a person do, and how it manifests itself in observable ways. Yet Spinoza provides all the necessary elements to make sense easily of the idea, allowing one not only to grasp its full scope but also to see it at work everywhere: 'each *thing* . . .' For the conatus is the force of existence. It is, so to speak, the fundamental energy that inhabits bodies and sets them in motion. The conatus is the principle of the mobilisation of bodies. To exist is to act, namely, to deploy this energy. Whence comes this energy? To do full justice to that question would require an ontological commentary. But a good enough answer for our purpose, half evident and half contentious – and since the subject matter will be *human* affairs – is that the energy of the conatus is simply life. And, this time hewing closest to Spinoza, it is the energy of *desire*. To be is to be a being of desire. To exist is to desire, and therefore to be active in the pursuit of one's objects of desire. Indeed, the link between desire as the effectuation of effort for the sake of persevering in being and the setting in motion of the body is

---

1 Benedictus de Spinoza, *Ethics*, part III, proposition 6, in *A Spinoza Reader, The Ethics and Other Works*, trans. Edwin Curley, Princeton University Press, 1994. Henceforth *Ethics*, III, 6.

expressed synthetically by the very term *conatus*. The Latin verb *conor,* from which it derives, means 'to undertake' [*entreprendre*] in the most general sense of 'to begin'. Like 'impetus', and likewise borrowed from the physics of the Renaissance, the conatus designates the thrust that changes the condition of something from rest to motion, the fundamental energy that shakes up the body and sets it on the course of pursuing some object. The history of each society is what both gives rise and sets limits to the range of undertakings [*entreprises*] that are possible within it, that is, to the range of objects of desire that a society considers legitimate. Free enterprise, in the most general sense of the freedom to undertake – that is, in the sense of the conatus – is consequently nothing other than the freedom to desire and to set out in pursuit of one's desire. That is why, outside the restrictions a society deems it appropriate to stipulate, free enterprise enjoys a kind of a priori obviousness. Noting the legitimacy of the production of material goods, the entrepreneurial lament – this time using the specifically capitalist meaning of the expression – repeatedly draws on this source in order to challenge any imposition of limits on 'free enterprise': 'I have a desire that conforms to the division of labour and I am prevented from pursuing it.' In this reproachful invocation of the freedom of enterprise, the entrepreneur is merely asserting the thrust of his or her conatus. And it is true that in the context of the ontologically desiring and active temperament of each being, and within the aforementioned limits, this freedom is incontestable.

THE DESIRE TO MAKE OTHERS DO SOMETHING: BOSSING AND ENLISTMENT

It is rather the freedom to recruit other powers [*puissances*] in the pursuit of one's personal desire that is not evident a priori. Very often, however, the combined effect of human ambition and the depth of the division of labour is that desires for material production have to be pursued collectively, thus, in a strictly etymological sense, *collaboratively*. This is where the employment relation is born: the employment relation is the totality of structural facts (those of the double separation) and juridical codifications that make it possible for some to involve others in the realisation of their own *enterprise*. It is thus a relation of *enlisting* [*enrôlement*], the essence of which is to make other powers of acting join in the pursuit of one's own industrial desire.

However, since it is a desire, an enterprise – both in general and specifically the productive, capitalist enterprise – can only arise, and can only be assumed, in the first person. The entrepreneur's exclamation is thus essentially reducible to an 'I feel like doing something.' Well then, great! Do it! But do it on your own – if you can. If that is not possible, the problem changes completely. The legitimacy of wanting to do something does not extend to wanting to make other people do it. Hence the ambitious development of the enterprise to the point that it necessitates *collaborations* requires a fully independent answer to the question of the forms that these collaborations should take. The issue here is that of the political participation of individuals in the organisation of the collective productive processes and the appropriation of the products of their common activity; in other words, it is the issue of *capture* by the subject of the master-desire.

From the standpoint of capture, it appears therefore that *enlistment* is the more general category, of which employment is only a particular case. One can however choose to name the containing concept after one that is contained by it. Thus it is possible to use the term *bossing* [*patronat*] to refer in the most general way to the relation within which master-desires engage the power of acting of enlistees in their enterprise: military commanders, in their conquests;

crusaders, in their crusades; sovereigns, in their sovereign power [*puissance*] (which is not theirs but belongs to the multitude); and capitalist business-owners, in their profits and dreams of industrial fulfilment. In the most general sense, *bossing* is a relation of *capturing*, instances of which are found in many areas outside that of the capitalist exploitation that gives it its primary signification today: the NGO directors appropriating the lion's share of the results of the activities of their activists; the university mandarins, of their juniors; the artists, of their assistants – all this outside the capitalist enterprise, and in pursuit of things that have nothing to do with monetary gain. They are no less *bosses* for that, specific inflections of the boss in general, capturers of the effort (conatus) of their *subordinates* enlisted in the service of a master-desire.

INTEREST, DESIRE, SETTING IN MOTION

Capture presupposes getting bodies to set themselves in motion in the service of the capturer *Mobilising* is therefore its constitutive preoccupation. For it is ultimately quite strange that people should so 'accept' to occupy themselves in the service of a desire that was not originally their own. Only the force of habit, resulting from the omnipresence of the bossing relations under which we live, can make us lose sight of the immense amount of social labour that is required for producing this 'setting oneself in motion for another' on such large scales. But the formal identity of the enlistment relation, considered at a certain level of abstraction, takes nothing away from the specificity of the contents and structures of its various inflections: the capitalist bosses have their own particular 'methods', which are not the same as those of the crusading bosses or the university bosses. And the capitalist method is *first of all* money. But is this not a well-known triviality?

Undoubtedly it is; but the banality of the experience it evokes does nothing to diminish its depth. And perhaps the capitalist bossing, despite its particularities, is the one best suited for the task of demonstrating what bossing as such 'runs on': it runs on interest – *namely*, on desire. Here we could paraphrase Spinoza: *interesse sive appetitus*. Some do not like this identity, however.[2] Or rather, they do not like its consequences. For if human essence is desiring, it follows from this identity that all actions must be considered *interested*. 'What is left then of the warmth of true relationships and nobility of feeling?' ask the defenders of the disinterested gift. Everything and nothing. Nothing if we stubbornly cling to the idea of a pure altruism, a movement out of the self in which the self maintains no stake. Everything, provided that we resist the reductive understanding of 'interest' that limits it to utilitarian calculations only. Interest is the obtainment of satisfaction; it is therefore another name for the object of desire, and is likewise infinitely varied. Is it at all possible to deny that we are *interested in our desires*? And if not, how then to refuse the status of interest to all the objects of desire that fall outside the range of merely economic desires? How to deny that there is interest in the gratitude that is expected for a gift, in the anticipation of reciprocity in love, in displays of largesse, in cashing in the symbolic profits of greatness or of a reputation for charity, just as much as in keeping a balance of profits and losses, but, 'simply', in a form other than that of the explicit calculation? It is true however that another desire, and a particularly strong one, the desire for enchantment, keeps impelling us to deny the

---

2   In particular the theoreticians of MAUSS, the Anti-Utilitarian Movement in the Social Sciences, who strive to show that humans are not only interested beings but can also assume the figure of *homo donator*, disinterested and altruistic. For a controversy over this issue, see Frédéric Lordon, 'Le don tel qu'il est et non qu'on voudrait qu'il fût', and Falafil, 'Quel paradigme du don? En clé d'intérêt ou en clé de don? Réponse à Frédéric Lordon', in 'De l'anti-utilitarisme. Anniversaire, bilan et controverses', *Revue du MAUSS semestrielle* 27 (2006).

existence of interests, as if the defenders of disinterest became the victims of the very utilitarian reduction that they set out to combat. Having committed themselves to the stirring task of stemming the icy tide of calculation, they have limited the application of the word *interest* to their enemy for the sole reason that this is how economic theory and utilitarian philosophy use the term. They thus incur the twofold cost of validating the designation, thus ratifying the reduction, and of relinquishing in that very gesture, for no good reason, the breadth of a concept with so much wider potential.[3] Yet, whichever path it chooses – including paths that pass through all possible and imaginable others – the effort of persevering in being as desire is never pursued except in the first person. Hence the pursuers must necessarily be considered interested, even when their desire is the desire to give, to help, to pay attention, or to show concern. The generality of desire therefore has room for the full gamut of interests, ranging from the self-declared economic interest, a historically constructed expression of interest as it *self-consciously* recognises itself in the form of accounting in monetary units, via all the forms of interest that are embedded in strategies with varying degrees of self-awareness, up to its least economic forms, indeed the most anti-economic, such as moral, symbolic, or psychological interests. Yet capitalist social relations draw much more widely from this range than a merely economistic reading would conceive. It does not follow that a conceptually unified account of these relations is impossible; but developing one would require having at our disposal, evidently, a unifying concept: the conatus, for example, that desiring force at the root of all interests, that interest-desire at the root of every servitude.

---

3   See Frédéric Lordon, *L'intérêt souverain. Essai d'anthropologie économique spinoziste*, La Découverte, 2006.

BARE LIFE AND MONEY

It is true that of all the desires it harnesses, capitalism begins with money – or rather with bare life, life in need of reproduction. For, in a decentralised economy with a division of labour, material reproduction passes through the gateway of money. This mediation is not purely a capitalist invention: the division of labour, and the monetary market exchange that accompanies it as it deepens beyond a certain threshold, have developed slowly over centuries. Capitalism inherited this layering of markets that evolved over the long term. But it could only truly take form by closing off the last avenues of independent individual or (small-scale) collective production, thus raising material heteronomy to an unprecedented level. The *full* dependence on the market division of labour is its condition of possibility. Marx and Polanyi among others have amply shown how the conditions for proletarianisation emerged, notably through the enclosure of the commons. In the wake of that act of the most complete, organised immiseration, people were left with only one option, the sale of their undifferentiated labour-power.

It is tedious to have to repeat such trivial and obvious facts, yet necessary inasmuch as contemporary fictions, built on 'work enrichment', 'participative management', 'employee empowerment' and other programmes of 'self-realisation' are successfully erasing the memory of that original truth about the employment relation: that it is a relation of dependence, a relation between agents in which one holds the conditions for the material reproduction of the other, and that this is the permanent backdrop and the immoveable foundation for anything that unfolds on top of it. Without being reducible to it, the employment relation is only possible when the mediation of money becomes the obligatory gateway, the exclusive gateway, through which the basal desire for material reproduction must pass. As employees repeatedly discover, all the incentives that the capitalist employment relation successively put on stage in order to enrich its scenery and elicit more refined interests in the workplace – interests such as advancement, socialising, 'fulfilment' – can collapse at any moment, leaving only the indestructible foundation of material dependence, a stark backdrop of menace hanging over life newly made bare.

Since the mediation of money functions as an obligatory gateway, the dependence on the provider of money is inscribed in the strategies of material reproduction from the outset, and as its most fundamental fact. Yet in a capitalist economy there are only two providers of money: the employer and the financier. For the employee, it is the employer; later it will also be the banker, but only marginally and on condition of a repayment capacity backed by pre-existing remuneration. Pushed to its limit, material heteronomy – namely, the inability to independently supply the necessities of one's reproduction as labour-power (and simply as life), and therefore the need to participate in the market division of labour – makes access to money imperative and money the cardinal object of desire, the desire that conditions all or almost all others. Money, writes Spinoza in one of the rare passages in which he addresses economics, has become a 'digest of everything', and 'that is why its image usually occupies the mind of the multitude more than anything else. For they can imagine hardly any species of joy without the accompanying idea of money as its cause.'[4] Spinoza by no means excluded himself from the common lot with this sharp observation.[5] Before engaging in philosophy,

---

4   *Ethics*, IV, Appendix 28. [The translation here follows the French translation of *Ethics*. (Trans.)]

5   And a distinction should be made between the 'common lot' that is unable to escape the necessities of material reproduction through the exchange of money, and the 'multitude', defined by the fact that its spirit is occupied by the image of money 'more than anything else'.

he had to polish lenses. A citizen of the United Provinces at the height of their economic power, he was well placed to identify the mutations that the deepening of the division of labour and the market-based organisation of material reproduction induced in the order of desires and collective affects: money, as the almost exclusive mediation of material strategies, 'the digest of everything', became the object of meta-desire – the obligatory gateway through which all other (market) desires must pass.

CURRENCY-RELATION, MONEY-DESIRE

Incidentally, this is the moment to make a conceptual distinction between two terms, *currency* and *money*, that are intuitively grasped as interchangeable and which few see the utility of disentangling. Why then have two words for a single thing? Pepita Ould-Ahmed, one of the first to properly examine this lexical difference, very correctly sees in it the effect of distinctive disciplinary appropriations – money for the anthropologists (and sociologists), currency for the economists – and ultimately a mere variation in perspective relative to what remains fundamentally one and the same object.[6] We can however extend this analysis, and qualify this 'variation in perspective' conceptually by making currency the name of a certain social relation, and money the name of the desire to which this relation gives birth.

Michel Aglietta and André Orléan made the decisive contribution of refuting the substantial (intrinsic value) and the functional (convenient means of exchange) approaches to understanding currency, seeing it rather as a *social relation*, buttressed in institutions, and as complex as the social

---

6 Pepita Ould-Ahmed, 'Monnaie des anthropologues, argent des économistes : à chacun le sien?', in E. Baumann, L. Bazin, P. Ould-Ahmed, P. Phélinas, M. Selim, R. Sobel (eds), *L'argent des anthropologues, la monnaie des économistes*, L'Harmattan, 2008.

relation of *capital*. [7] <u>Currency is thus not a value in itself but the operator of value.</u> Above all, it is fundamentally the effect of a collective belief in its efficacy as a means of repayment, since everyone justifies accepting the monetary sign by the fact that everyone else is equally and reciprocally willing to accept it. The production of this common acceptance of a sign, which is ultimately perfectly arbitrary since it lacks any intrinsic value, is the monetary question par excellence. This *essentially fiduciary* nature of currency, long occluded by the illusions of metallic fetishism, must be brought to light if one is to grasp that it has no substantial character and is fundamentally *interpersonal* – in other words, that at the scale of the whole society it is a social relation. Monetary institutions have no other function than to produce and reproduce that social relation of shared recognition and trust which, attached to some sign, establish it as a universally accepted means of payment. [8] Currency is only (re-)produced, or destroyed, together with this relation. That is why, far from being reducible to dyadic interactions, money imposes itself (when it imposes itself) with a sovereign force, and at the level of the whole community whose collective power it in some way expresses. [9]

If currency is the means of payment as a social relation,

---

7   Michel Aglietta and André Orléan, *La violence de la monnaie*, PUF, 1982; (eds), *La monnaie entre violence et confiance*, Odile Jacob, 2002; (eds), *La monnaie souveraine*, Odile Jacob, 1998.

8   On the forms of monetary confidence and their institutional armatures, see Bruno Théret, 'La monnaie au prisme de ses crises d'hier et d'aujourd'hui', in B. Théret (ed.), *La monnaie dévoilée par ses crises*, Éditions de l'EHESS, 2007.

9   On the idea of the sovereignty of the currency as manifestation of the power of the community, see Frédéric Lordon and André Orléan, 'Genèse de l'État et genèse de la monnaie: le modèle de la *potentia multitudinis*', in Y. Citton and F. Lordon, *Spinoza et les sciences sociales. De la puissance de la multitude à l'économie des affects*, Éditions Amsterdam, 2008.

money is currency grasped from the standpoint of the subjects, namely, currency as object of desire – this 'digest of everything' without whose 'accompanying idea as cause no joy exists'. Money is the subjective expression, in the form of desire, of the monetary social relation. This social relation produces the common acceptance of the monetary sign and therefore turns it – from the perspective of individuals – into an object of desire, or meta-desire, since this particular object is the general equivalent that gives access to all (material) objects of desire. This relation and its institutional framework is thus responsible for producing one of the most powerful attractors of an economy of desire structured by the commodity. We can clearly see here both the difference between, and the complementary nature of, the respective analytical registers of currency and money: on the one hand, the institutional and social mechanisms that produce a collective belief-trust, and on the other, the mystification of individual desire. What is undoubtedly needed is not to disqualify one perspective with the help of the other, but rather to use both together in order to take full stock of the monetary object, exactly in the manner of Bourdieu's objection to the false antinomy between objectivism and subjectivism.[10] The former is only interested in structures, dismissing agents as their merely passive bearers, whereas the latter ignores structures on the ground that nothing exists except the lived experience of individuals; both are thus equally incapable of thinking the *expression* of structures in and through the individual psyche, namely, the presence of structures inside the subjects themselves, but in the form of dispositions, desires, beliefs and affects.

---

10   Pierre Bourdieu, *Choses dites*, Minuit, 1987.

THERE IS NO SUCH THING AS VOLUNTARY SERVITUDE

Dependence on the object of desire 'money' is the bedrock of employees' enlistment, the unacknowledged purpose of all work contracts, and the backdrop of menace known to the employee as much as to the employer. The setting-in-motion of employed bodies 'in the service of . . .' takes its energy from the fixation of the conatus-desire on the money object, of which capitalist structures have established the employer as the sole provider. If the primary meaning of domination consists in one agent's having to pass through another to access the object of desire, then evidently the employment relation is a relation of domination. But, first, the intensity of domination is directly proportional to the intensity of the desire of the dominated over which the dominator has control. And second, once primitive accumulation created the structural conditions for radical material heteronomy – which all the subsequent evolution of capitalism seeks to further deepen – money accedes to the top of the hierarchy of objects of desire-interest; it is the one object on which the pursuit of all other desires depends – including non-material ones. 'The first premise of all human existence and, therefore, of all history, [is] the premise, namely, that men must be in a position to live in order to be able to "make history." But life involves before everything else eating and drinking, a habitation, clothing and many other things.'[11] Thus, in the monetary economy with division of labour that characterises capitalism, no desire is more imperious than the desire for money, and consequently, no hold is more powerful than that of enlistment through employment.

Revisiting this type of obvious fact is manifestly necessary

---

11   Karl Marx and Friedrich Engels, 'The German Ideology', in *The German Ideology including Theses on Feuerbach*, Prometheus Books, 1998, p. 47.

for refuting the idea of 'voluntary servitude', that oxymoron that is often presented today as the key to understanding the employment relation and its recent and most troubling manipulative evolution. Would it be fair however to say that La Boétie's argument is better than his book's title? To the extent that it is, one could add that what is amazing is the precocity of an expression that distils ahead of its time, not only all the aporiae of the subjectivist metaphysics that feed contemporary individualistic thinking, but also the actual manner in which individuals intuitively relate to themselves. The individual-subject imagines itself to be a free being, endowed with an autonomous will, whose actions are the effects of its sovereign volition: hence, had I wanted emancipation strongly enough, I would have been able to escape my condition of servitude; consequently, if I am in this condition, it must be the fault of my will, and my servitude has to be voluntary. Under such a metaphysics of subjectivity, voluntary servitude is doomed to remain an insoluble enigma. How can one 'want' to be in a state that is so manifestly undesirable? Absent an illumination of this mystery, the evocation of voluntary servitude, which captures the tension of an aspiration to liberty that inexplicably persists in remaining unfulfilled, can go no further politically than a call for raising consciousness. While that is already no bad thing, what it is absolutely incapable of producing is a causal understanding of this non-fulfilment.

One among many other relations of domination, the employment relation as the capture of a certain desire (individuals striving to secure their biological-material perseverance's desire for money) exposes in all its nakedness how enslavement really works: through the necessity and the intensity of a desire. To rescue from this argument a rehabilitated idea of 'voluntary servitude' one would have to argue that we are fully in charge of our desires. But in this respect, the case of the employment relation has the merit of pointing out the existence of desires that assert themselves in ways that have nothing to do with free choice – otherwise one would also have to speak of voluntary servitude in the case of someone threatened with a gun, since such a person would obey any order because of the (powerful) desire not to die, captured (the person and the desire) by the hostage-taker. It is the social structures, in the case of employment, those of the capitalist relations of production, that configure desires and predetermine the strategies for attaining them. Within the structures of radical material heteronomy, the desire for persevering biologically-materially is narrowed down [*déterminé*] to the desire for money, which is in turn narrowed down to the desire to be employed.

But while the example of employment is useful for making patent the heteronomy of the desire associated with it, to remain confined to its particularity would have the opposite effect. No one strove to establish the absolute generality of the heteronomy of desire more than Spinoza. Ontologically speaking, the conatus, generic desiring force and 'man's very essence',[12] is first of all pure momentum, and has no definite direction. In the words of Laurent Bove, it is a 'desire without an object.'[13] It finds objects to pursue soon enough, but they will be indicated to it from outside. For one catches a desire in the encounters with things, memories of things, and all the associations that unfold from these events that Spinoza calls *affections*. '*Desire* is man's very essence, insofar as it is conceived to be determined, from any given affection of it, to do something.' The wording here is no less obscure than in the case of the perseverance in being, yet it says exactly what must be understood: human essence, which is the power of activity – but generic and, as such, intransitive,

---

12   *Ethics*, III, Definitions of the Affects I.
13   Laurent Bove, '*Éthique*, partie III,' in Pierre-François Moreau and Charles Ramond (eds), *Lectures de Spinoza*, Ellipses, 2006.

a pure force of desire but as yet aimless – only becomes a directed activity due to the effect of a prior affection – something that happens to it and modifies it. It is the affection that points the desire in a particular direction and gives it an object for its concrete exertion. From this follows a radical reversal of the ordinary understanding of desire as the pull of a pre-existing, desirable object. It is rather the push of the conatus that invests things and institutes them as objects of desire.[14] And these investments are entirely determined by the interplay of affects.

An affection, something that happens; an affect, which is the effect, sad or joyful, of that affection; the feeling that follows of wanting to do something, to possess, to run away, to destroy, to pursue, or whatever it may be. The life of desire unfolds in its entirety from this elementary sequence. It unfolds most often through the interplay of memory and associations, for the affections and the affects that result from them leave traces that are more or less deep, more or less amenable to being remobilised.[15] Old joys and sorrows contaminate new objects that are related to them, which then become new objects of desire.[16] Does not Swann fall in love with Odette for the sole reason that she reminds him of a beloved, delicate beauty in a Botticelli fresco? And when desire does not pass from one object to another through association and recollection, it circulates between individuals who induce each other to desire through the mutual spectacle of

---

14   *Ethics*, III, 9, Scholium.

15   On the importance of the traceable body, the body that keeps traces (*vestigia*) as the support of memory, and on the vestigial causality of the affective life, the work of reference is Lorenzo Vinciguerra, *Spinoza et le signe. Genèse de l'imagination*, Vrin, 2005.

16   *Ethics*, III, 15, Corollary: 'From this alone – that we have regarded a thing with an affect of joy or sadness, of which it is not itself the efficient cause, we can love it or hate it.'

their passions.[17] This occurs less within strictly dyadic relations than through mediations that are essentially social, and
the source of the huge variety of emulations of desire: I love
because he loves; or, if she loves, then I love less, or indeed
more. Or I hate, precisely because he loves! (As we know, one
social group's taste can be another's bad taste, and so the desire
of the former to pursue something spurs the latter to avoid it,
for example.)

An exploration of the infinite convolutions of passionate
life according to Spinoza would be a book in itself.[18] What is
important here is to emphasise the profound heteronomy of
desire and affects, caught up in the vagaries of past and present
encounters, and the dispositions for recollecting, linking, and
imitating formed over the long course of (social) biographical
trajectories – above all, there is in this absolutely nothing to
suggest an autonomous will, sovereign control, or free self-
determination. The passionate life imposes itself on individuals
and they are chained to it for better or worse, prey to the fortunes
of encounters that cheer or sadden them, its real causes – the
key to understanding it – forever escaping their grasp. To be
sure, Spinoza writes an *Ethics*, outlining a trajectory for liberation, one that may be embarked on, as it happens, with no
deliberate decision.[19] The liberated, however, are few – have we
ever encountered a single one? As for the common lot, the title
of the fourth part of the *Ethics* sets the tone unambiguously: *Of
Human Servitude, or the Powers of the Affects*. Similarly in the
first two sentences of the foreword: 'Man's lack of power to
moderate and restrain the affects I call servitude. For the man
who is subject to the affects is under the control, not of himself,
but of fortune . . .' Given the fortuitous order of encounters and

17   Ibid., III, 27.
18   See Alexandre Matheron, *Individu et communauté chez Spinoza*,
Minuit, 1988.
19   Pascal Sévérac, *Le devenir actif chez Spinoza*, Honoré Champion, 2005.

the laws of the affective life through which these encounters (affections) produce their effects, human beings are passionate automata.

Subjectivist-individualist thought, built around the idea of free will as sovereign self-control, predictably rejects this verdict of radical heteronomy *in toto* and to its last breath. It is indeed this rejection that is expressed – prospectively in La Boétie, almost in embodied form today – in the idea of 'voluntary servitude', since, without the outright duress of physical restraint, one would not have submitted to being chained unless one more or less wanted it, however mysterious that 'wanting' is bound to remain. Against this insoluble aporia, Spinoza proposes an altogether different mechanism of alienation: the real chains are those of our affects and desires. There is no such thing as voluntary servitude. There is only passionate servitude. That, however, is universal.

THE ASYMMETRY OF THE MONETARY INITIATIVE

That the necessity of material-biological persistence is experienced as an 'imposition' or a 'chore', and therefore perceived as incompatible with the emotional tenor commonly associated with the upsurge and transport of desire, merely reveals the limits of intuition based on everyday experience. Conceptually speaking, in no way does it subtract this necessity from the range of desires. We really do take great pains to acquire the things we deem necessary for our reproduction. Suffice it to observe with what ferocity, up to and including violence, people pursue such things when they are lacking (for example in cases of grave penury, natural catastrophe, etc.). Thus it is indeed on this very first desire that enlistment through employment relies. As the provider of money within the capitalist social structure, the employer holds the key to the basal desire, the desire to survive, which is hierarchically above and the condition for all other desires, making the latter, by definition, also subordinate to the employer.

One may object that the strategic situation of dependence is more symmetrical than that, since the employer too seeks an object of desire that the employee possesses: labour-power. But the employer needs *indefinite* labour-power rather than that of a specific employee, for the disparity between the number of employers and the number of employees (arising from the very fact that the process of production is collective) makes labour-power fungible, at least within the same set of competences: from the point of view of the employer, *this one* (this quantity of labour power) will do as well as *that one*. The fungibility that allows employers to draw indefinite labour-power from the undifferentiated population of the employable is thus the first factor that reduces to modest proportions the formal symmetry between capital and labour in their relation of mutual dependence. The second is their respective ability to hold out without the other. Whichever is less able to defer obtaining the object of desire that is in the other's possession will fall under the other's domination. But as the rarity and the hazards of employee revolts indirectly attest, it is capital that can afford to wait things out. In contrast, individual labour-power must reproduce itself daily. Blocking its access to money is fatal to it within a very short time, and can only be resisted through various forms of organised employee solidarity. Thus although one can say that, *formally*, to produce anything the providers of machines need the providers of labour as much as the providers of labour need the providers of machines, the entire *real* strategic situation that results from their relation, as determined by the social structures of capitalism, distorts the initial symmetry and turns it into a relation of dependence, and therefore into domination.

As for the distribution of agents between the respective

positions of capitalists and workers within the social structure of capitalism, it is decided upstream, and through the same strategic question of access to money. The capitalists, providers of money to the employees, must likewise find their own suppliers, and moreover on a considerably larger scale, since they need to finance the whole cycle of production in advance (working capital requirements). The supplier of money to the capitalist is the banker. But the banker only supplies limited leverage, in the form of a debt supplement that must be added to an already constituted net capital stock. It is the ability to organise a first round of financing and amass a base of net equity that selects from among the 'candidates' those who will hold the position of the capitalist. Although 'candidacy' is a poor choice of word, since those who own nothing but their labour-power, and only have access to money *after* having sold it, precisely where what counts is to show that one is capable of paying *in advance*, are never in the running to begin with. If we understand by 'finance' the full set of mechanisms that allow agents to (temporarily) spend more than they earn, it is the ability to access money in the non-wage form of finance that identifies the potential capitalist. The fundamental difference is that money as wages is accessed in the form of *flow*, namely, in quantities that allow for the short-term reproduction of labour-power but do not allow a glimpse beyond this limited horizon, whereas money as financing is accessed in the form of *stock*, namely, with the hope of crossing the critical threshold of the process of accumulation by self-sustaining valorisation (in which capital grows by itself, thanks to its capacity to extract surplus-value). Thus the capitalist has privileged access to *money-capital*, rather than simply to money.

The character of Antoine Doinel in the film *The 400 Blows*, who, seeking the means for his material reproduction after having broken with family and school, briefly entertains the idea of going into business, gives his companion a dazzling shorthand exposition of the obstacles facing the prospective capitalist: 'It's a question of cash at the start', a synthetic proposition that captures the imperative of having access to money – considered as the strategic stake ('it is a question of . . .') – but crucially *ex ante*, in the form of the monetary advance ('at the start'), namely, as a stock of money-capital, and not as an *ex post* remuneration for labour-power whose reproduction requires spending the money on consumption, thus making it impossible to see beyond. Antoine Doinel is so conscious of the necessity of having this stock at his disposal *first* that, having nothing, he considers stealing some furniture from his friend's father in order to convert it into money-capital, thus intuitively making the connection between the preliminary stock and the initial theft, and discovering – in practice for himself, as a revelation for the viewer – the original robbery of primitive accumulation. To speak tautologically, or to use a ballistic metaphor, one needs a launcher to 'launch' a business. One needs an initial amount (of energy/start-up capital) in order to be propelled past the critical threshold – the capitalist equivalent of escape velocity. From this follows a fundamental inequality with respect to the social capacity of individuals to pursue a capitalist desire to do something. Only those who hold the monetary initiative in the form of a stock of money can devote themselves to a career that combines their material reproduction with doing what they want, sometimes even with the constitution of a fortune. The rest are held down by the gravitational pull of their mere reproduction, confined to the horizon of the basal desire, a desire that conditions everything but counts for nothing, because it is only the prerequisite for the pursuit of other desires deemed worthier of attainment. It is as if the true order of desire (from the point of view of individuals) only begins past the satisfaction of this basal desire, for which the only solution society offers is to be enlisted through employment.

DOMINATION AT EVERY LEVEL

The landscape of domination is nevertheless more complex than it appears in the light of the bipolar antagonism that Marx analysed. As a result of the deepening of specialisation and the internal division of labour, the face-off between the owner-boss and the mass of labourers supervised by a few foremen has given way to increasingly layered organisational structures. The hierarchical chain of command includes an ever-growing number of intermediate levels that diffract the primary relation of domination into a myriad of secondary ones. At every level of the chain, agents experience the employment relation ambivalently as subordinated-subordinating, each both receiving orders and giving orders to others. Thus the canonical form of the relation that opposes a dominator (or a small number of dominators) to the mass of the dominated explodes into multiple, hierarchical, interlocking dependencies that paint a kind of continuous gradient of domination.

If La Boétie's argument is infinitely better than the title of his book, it is here that it best manifests its merit. For, having suggested the idea of a habitus of servitude that leads nations, through slow inurement, to live their submission as an ordinary condition, La Boétie insists on the role of chains of dependence along which individuals are kept in place separate from each other by their interests. From the sovereign, through concentric circles of subordinates of successive ranks, and down to the lowest levels of the social hierarchy, favours and advantages that are often vital trickle down – symbolically and existentially in the higher strata, materially in the lower ones. What La Boétie shows is therefore a *hierarchical structure of servitude*, and it is difficult to imagine how any particular 'will' would be in a position to overturn it, since the domination that takes place at each of its levels is all the more intense when the local dominators are also dominated and brought to despair through their own dependence. La Boétie's image of society as a whole, converging on the sovereign as the ultimate source of favour, and held together at all levels through the interplay of interest-desires, also applies to the large business enterprise, a layered hierarchy that structures the passionate servitude of the employed multitude on a gradient of dependence. Every employee wants something, and that something depends on the approval of superiors, who likewise strive to pursue their own will, to which they subordinate their subordinates, creating an ascending chain of dependence to which corresponds a descending chain of instrumentalisation.

Perhaps Norbert Elias is, in his own way, an heir of La Boétie.[20] In any case, the idea of chains of dependence holds a central place in his thinking. It is indeed from their lengthening and intensification, expressions of the deepening of the division of labour and the 'densification' of social life, that the principal incentives to regulate one's individual conduct emerge, to both curb the tendency to yield to fits of temper and inculcate concentration and calculation. For to storm out is now the surest way to lose the coveted goods – it is to storm out of the relation with those through whom the pursuit of these goods passes. Compromises and intertemporal trade-offs are the patterns of actions slowly instilled through training in this new relational context characterised by drawn-out strategic mediations. 'Strategic mediation' signifies here that the path from the desiring subject to the desired object is ever less direct and passes through ever more intermediaries, who must all be respected or at least managed. Incidentally, one must take care to avoid understanding the idea of strategy in an overtly conscious or calculating sense – although this sense should not

20   See Norbert Elias, *The Civilizing Process: Sociogenetic and Psychogenetic Investigations*, Blackwell, 2000.

be excluded, of course. But if we choose to call strategic a set of actions concatenated for the purpose of reaching a desired end, we must concede that these concatenations can just as well be produced by ways of doing things that are incorporated to the point of no longer being consciously aimed, relying on almost automatic modes – exactly that which Bourdieu calls habitus.

By strategic one should rather understand, more fundamentally, *the very logic of desire* and the full range of ways in which it cuts itself a path, whether these ways follow from calm calculation or from conduct governed by affects.[21] Laurent Bove is therefore caught in no contradiction when he speaks of 'strategies of the conatus,'[22] even as the Spinozist philosophy of action radically breaks with the model of the sovereign, calculating decision (but is fully capable of including it as one of its very particular cases, which is not for that matter an exception to the overall logic of the passionate life, as a superficial reading might suggest).

AMBIENT PRESSURES AND RISING VIOLENCE (COMPETITION AND SHAREHOLDER PRESSURE)

The hierarchical architecture of dependence through employment is highly sensitive to the surrounding stress and the intensity of local relations changes according to variations in external pressures. If initially, and by extension, we treat as 'external' the pressure that arises at the very top of the hierarchical chain, any intensification that takes place there cascades down the structure, straining all its levels successively. At each rung, the

21   A false antinomy (between 'calculation' and 'affects') par excellence, Frédéric Lordon, 'Homo Passionalis OEconomicus', *Actes de la Recherche en Sciences Sociales*, conference paper given at 'Economie et fabrique de la subjectivité', Association française de psychiatrie, Paris, 2010.
22   Laurent Bove, *La stratégie du conatus. Affirmation et résistance chez Spinoza*, Vrin, 1996.

desire to keep the advantages associated with one's own position can only be satisfied at the price of a supplementary effort
exacted by the rung above. Everything else remaining equal, the
probability of success diminishes. The injunction coming from
on high and propagating through the thick of the system
diffuses in that very propagation an effect of fear, that 'incon-
stant sadness, born of the idea of a future or past, things whose
outcome we to some extent doubt.'[23] By the very logic of desire,
fear and hope are its nearly permanent backdrop once taking
hold of the object is postponed, and the time that separates
desire from fulfilment 'necessarily' creates (from the point of
view of the agent) some uncertainty. This temporal tension in
desire gives the pursuit of its object its ambivalent passionate
coloration (*fluctuatio animi*, the vacillation of the mind, as
Spinoza calls it), since the joyful affect of hope (success) is (logically) accompanied by the sad affect of fear (failure). The 'external' conditions under which individuals pursue their desires
determine the particular balance between hope and fear in each
case, hence the dominant affective tonality that accompanies
their effort. In the context of employment, the desire for advantage becomes wrapped in fear when its attainment depends on
strategies with decreasing probabilities of success – such as
reaching an intermediate goal that seems to grow increasingly
distant. The combination of the steady intensity of desire – for
the employee, access to money remains as imperative as ever,
and giving up is not an option – and the growing difficulty of
the conditions of its fulfilment generates a tension characterised by the sad affect of fear. Furthermore, as all sad affects do,
this fear induces in the conatus a surplus of activity as it tries to
overcome it: 'the greater the sadness, the greater is the part of
the man's power of acting to which it is necessarily opposed.'[24]

---

23 *Ethics*, III, Definitions of the Affects XIII.
24 Ibid., III, 37, Demonstration.

This passionate situation, determined by the general structure of enlistment through the employment relation and by the ambient conditions under which the relation takes effect, imposes itself on agents without recourse and prescribes all their efforts, which are deployed with an intensity proportional to that of the commanding desire. But the intensification of the movements of the conative power in a general context of domination and instrumentalisation is necessarily accompanied by an increase in the level of violence against others – those whom the agent is capable of dominating/instrumentalising – as well as against oneself, for that matter.

The reorientation of corporate governance towards maximizing shareholder value – namely, the demand from 'above' to extract a rate of return on net capital far beyond the prevailing norms of Fordist capitalism[25] – provides a textbook example of the propagation of violence that may follow from the straining of the chain of dependence throughout the organisation. The brutal and purely quantitative increase in short-term targets is in itself sufficient cause for the intensification of the relations of instrumentalisation and their intrinsic violence. The hierarchical organisation of the division of labour transmits the impulse from one end of the chain of dependence to the other, converting the economic abstraction of the rate of return on capital into concrete violence in the process. As it descends from top to bottom, the commanding desire for financial returns is translated at each rung into short-term desires/targets, while the captured product of efforts moves up in the opposite direction in order to be totalised as an overall rise in productivity, promptly converted into yield for shareholders. The degree to which the impulse

---

25   The adjective 'Fordist' stands here for the regime of accumulation whose concept was developed by regulation theory. See Robert Boyer, *Regulation Theory: The State of the Art*, Routledge, 2002.

coming from above avoids transmission losses and maintains its *mobilising* power while traversing the thick of the organisation depends both on the internal structures of the latter and on its over-determination by external factors. Both have the effect and sometimes the purpose of raising the penalty for failure, and consequently of increasing fear, hence adding to the reactive power of acting that individuals deploy. This is the case for example with managerial reforms that block off avenues for collective resistance and condemn employees to meet crushing performance targets under the pressure of inescapable personal surveillance (reporting), or that establish internal competition and create job insecurity through the threat of demotion or dismissal.

Likewise, the external competitive context contributes to all these effects by exacerbating the struggles for persistence across the board. As the enterprise as a whole fights to stay in business, the degree of mobilisation necessary to avoid being wiped out by competitors 'imposes itself' according to the desire of its upper management, interested to the highest degree. But the firm can also export its own imperatives and thus gain from the competition between other firms that depend on it, namely, its suppliers. For, just as organisations are internally constituted in a hierarchical chain, so are the external relations between enterprises structured in chains of economic dependence. The violence of the relations of domination that pass through the supply chain is every bit the equal of that of other economic relations, as the upper management of second-tier companies, which only survive thanks to the patronage of one or a few large clients, know from experience. Unlike the employment relation, whose specific jurisprudence developed precisely in a break with the common law of contracts, the supplier relation is a pure market relation. But, when strained by competition, it hurls organisations against each other with a violence that reflects the vital importance to each of preserving major contracts. This is an almost canonical illustration of the conatus as effort of persevering in being: the organisations fight in order to not disappear, which says something about the intensity with which they sometimes pursue their goals – the hypostasis of the organisations ('they') refers in fact, first of all, to the conatus of upper management.

External violence thus incessantly produces internal violence, and vice versa. On the one hand, the organisation caught up in aggressive relations of competition translates this external pressure into internal mobilisation, the struggle against other organisations carried out through increasing the stress on its own employees. On the other hand, internal stress leads employees, should they have the option, to turn the pressure outwards; for example, purchasing departments are able to pass on to suppliers the pressure to raise productivity. Regarding this, one should listen to the testimony of a former small-company CEO, whose tongue was loosened by an early and golden retirement.[26] He describes the methods of these purchasing agents who deliberately assign communication with suppliers to young managers, freshly recruited and appointed, and therefore so much more vulnerable and so much more likely to exercise economic violence by demanding, with a brutality whose traumatic memory stays with the speaker, price reductions that amount to the almost full confiscation by the client of the supplier's productivity gains. But who has not heard about the tribulations of the suppliers to large retailers, or about the farmers who must deal with the food industry? As can be expected, agents – both collective and individual – caught up in relations of dependence and placed in situations where they are obliged to defend vital interests – economic survival for enterprises, keeping their

26 Documentary by Gilles Perret, *Ma mondialisation*, DVD, Les Films du Paradoxe, 2006.

jobs for employees – are driven to externalise the bulk of the effort required of them in any way they can, passing on the pressure to all those who depend on them. All of these structural facts – shareholder pressure, competition, labour market deregulation, managerial reforms of the organisation – have the effect of modifying the passionate situation of agents and the intensity with which they fight for their objects of desire. Violence therefore spreads along the chains of dependence within, as well as between, enterprises, freighted by radically raised stakes for all agents as a result of the intensification of ambient pressures, and according to the implacable logic that demands that the violence meted out be proportionate to the violence suffered.

JOYFUL MOBILISATION AND MARKET ALIENATION

If the question is mobilisation, in the most literal sense of knowing what makes bodies move – that is, what induces the energies of each conatus to do something or other and with a specific intensity – it must be conceded that the passionate landscape of capitalism is significantly more diverse than the preceding analysis revealed. Grasping it in the full variety of its affects is important, not only due to a kind of ethics of analysis, but primarily for understanding the causes of capitalism's endurance – for we can say that it too, in a way, exhibits an (astounding) tendency to persevere in its being. If employees accept the enlistment relation imposed on them by the social structure of capitalism, and submit to demands for ever-rising productivity, it is not only the effect of compulsion or organisational violence, but also because at times they get something out of it: opportunities for joy.

Evidently, a part of this something, indeed its very first element, is the satisfaction of the basal desire, the desire for material reproduction by way of access to money within a

monetary economy with a division of labour. Although
dulled by habit and diminished by all the pain associated
with the transaction, getting paid is the employment relation's joyful moment. The concept of 'joy' must be understood here with a certain analytical coldness, emptied of the
ideas of rapture, plenitude or jubilation that are commonly
associated with it. One can experience joy at all levels of
intensity, including very low ones, associated with the most
ordinary; it can even go unnoticed, lost within a larger
complex of affects that makes it hard to isolate. Once the
idea of joy is purged of all connotations of effervescence and
enthusiasm, it is perfectly correct to say that securing the
money that allows the satisfaction of the basal desire causes
joy – but in the same way that escaping death by becoming a
slave causes joy. However, one of the causes of capitalism's
longevity is its success in enriching the passionate complex
of the employment relation, notably by introducing other,
more straightforward occasions for joy, of which the best
known is of course attached to the growth of consumption.
Of all the factors at work in maintaining the relation of
employment dependence, market alienation with its characteristic affects is no doubt the strongest. Although confined
to a very narrow register, the proliferation of things to buy
provides desire with an infinite multiplication of points of
application. And the stage of mass consumption must be
reached for the full scope of the Spinozist statement 'they
can imagine hardly any species of joy without the accompanying idea of money as its cause' to become clear.[27] The
supreme deftness of capitalism, in this respect decisively the
product of the Fordist era, lay in using the expanded supply
of things to buy and the stimulation of demand to provoke
this reordering of desire, so that from then on the 'image [of

---

27 *Ethics*, IV, Appendix 28.

money] . . . occupie[d] the mind of the multitude more than anything else'.[28]

With its singular ability to fixate desire, the commodity raises dependence through employment to a higher level, but it also associates it with the joyous affects of monetary acquisition. Hence its deployment on an unprecedented scale counts as one of the great 'achievements' of a capitalism whose conative force so to speak reveals itself in its capacity to generate its own conditions of perseverance. By harnessing every form of the desire for things, the expanded access to commodities – whose debt to the structural historical transformations that regulation theory sums up under the name 'Fordism' must be reiterated[29] – entrenched a certain surrender of the idea of overthrowing capitalism. One need only note the (elementary) deftness with which the discourse that defends the established order dissociates the figure of the consumer from that of the employee, encouraging individuals to identify exclusively with the former while relegating the latter to the realm of incidental considerations. The justifications offered for contemporary transformations in employment practices – from longer work hours ('it allows stores to open on Sundays') to competition-enhancing deregulation ('it lowers prices') – always contrive to catch agents by 'the joyful affects' of consumption, appealing only to the consumer in them. The process of forming the European Union brought this strategy to the highest perfection by accomplishing the almost complete eviction of social legislation, replacing it with laws against unfair competition which were conceived and advertised as the greatest possible service to individuals – indeed as the only way to truly serve their well-being[30] – but

---

28   Ibid.

29   Boyer, *Regulation Theory*.

30   Contrary to the common non-sense of a French reading that unduly projects its own references, the 'social market economy', of German origin, which provides the theoretical model for the European Union, is in no way based on

solely addressing their social identity as consumers. This end-point must be put in historical perspective and then further connected to the 'historical success' of Fordism, to which is obviously owed the uplift of this figure of the consumer, which rose out of the figure of the wage-earner until it has almost completely replaced it, certainly within mainstream discourse, but also in a certain way within the psyches of individuals who perform at times staggering feats of compartmentalisation in this regard. For the mediations that link each person's wage-labour to his or her objects of consumption are so drawn-out and complex that everything works in favour of this disconnec-tion, and very few make the link between the gains they receive as consumers and the additional burden they bear as employees – and this, crucially, because the consumed objects have been produced by others, who are anonymous and too far away for the yoke of their employment to enter the consumers' conscious-ness and echo their own.

The whole system of market desire (marketing, media, advertising, the means of transmission of consumption norms) works therefore to consolidate the submission of individuals to the central relations of capitalism, since employment appears not only as the sole solution to the problem of material repro-duction, but also all the more attractive the more the range of objects offered to the acquisitive appetite expands indefinitely. This joyful alienation through commodities goes so far that it is willing to take on a few sad affects, those of indebtedness for

developing mechanisms for social security but rather on the improvement of the well-being of consumers through the intensification of competition: 'this orienta-tion towards consumption is effectively the equivalent of a social service provided by the market economy', writes Alfred Müller-Armack, adviser to Ludwig Erhard and the thinker of ordoliberalism (which is the intellectual basis of the EU), cited in Hans Tietmeyer, *Économie sociale de marché et stabilité monétaire*, Economica, 1999; see also François Denord and Antoine Schwartz, *L'Europe sociale n'aura pas lieu*, Éditions Raisons d'agir, 2009.

example, when the desired objects exceed the means of one's current income, yet are made tempting through credit mechanisms that compound dependence through employment with the obligation of future repayments. As we know, there is hardly a more powerful employment 'socialisation' mechanism than the mortgage of the 'young couple', bound to the necessity of employment for the next twenty years. One can get a sense of the intensity of this fixation by considering the role played by the fascination with opulence in the rejection of 'actually existing socialisms', the shimmering face of the commodity-inducing forces of desire fast converted into adherence to capitalism (regardless of subsequent disillusionments). One doubts therefore the long-term passionate viability of a social formation that would make the choice – for example, through de-growth – of a voluntary reduction in its material aspirations in isolation, while remaining exposed to the sight of its neighbours amassing objects, and consequently to all the stimulations brought about by the imitation of desire.[31] The intention here is not to conclude the impossibility of a historical bifurcation based on de-growth, but to emphasise the (demanding) passionate conditions of its possibility, and the necessity it would face of first constructing an imaginary, namely, an affective and desiring hermeneutics of a whole new world.

ENLISTMENT AS ALIGNMENT

Precisely because the determining effects of structures are deeply historical, the passionate configuration of employment mobilisation, being structurally determined, is itself prone to such historical transformations. The first regime of mobilisation, the one studied by Marx, relied on 'the spur of hunger'; it used the basal desire of material-biological reproduction to the

---

31 *Ethics*, III, 27.

last. This regime was replaced by the Fordist regime of mobilisation, with its joyful commodity alienation and its expanded access to consumption. Everything suggests that this regime is undergoing in turn a profound mutation, manifest in the new managerial methods of enlistment and the new affective sensibilities they are able to exploit. The passionate situation of employment is significantly enriched in the process, thwarting old forms of anti-capitalist critique, and providing new opportunities for losing one's way in the aporiae of 'voluntary servitude'.

The diffraction of the relation of dependence through the hierarchical structure of the enterprise has already considerably blurred the original landscape of capitalist domination. The 'bastard' case of the foreman, an employee who is also the delegate of the owner-boss's authority, had early on perturbed the pure, canonical representation of the face-off between capital and labour. With the deepening of the enterprise's internal division of labour, this perturbation has been generalised: even the top executives are employees. Marxist theory has long identified the problem, but without offering any truly satisfying solution, perhaps because it changed the question to one that was easier to answer: why do certain employees come to make common cause with capital? Why do they take its side? If employees set themselves in motion because of their desire for things they can buy, at least they are doing it for their own gain. But that they should enter into an active and sometimes even joyful relation of collaboration, and deliberately put all their energies into the service of capital – this is prima facie a mystery harder to understand. In any case, it is quite the supreme achievement from the point of view of bossing, considered as the relation of a power enlisting other powers.

For, generically speaking, mobilisation is a matter of co-linearity. The desire of the enlistees must be *aligned* with the master-desire. In other words, if the conatus to be enlisted is a force acting with a certain intensity, it must be given a 'correct' orientation, namely a direction that conforms to the direction of the boss's desire (whether the latter is an individual or an organisation). Since it is a question of direction and alignment, vectors offer an appropriate metaphor. The vector v is defined by a direction in space and an intensity (a real, positive number, using the notation $|\vec{v}|$). The enlistment of one conatus in the service of another can then be imagined by analogy as the scalar product of their two vectors: hence $\vec{d} \cdot \vec{D}$, $\vec{D}$ being the master-desire and $\vec{d}$ the enlisted conatus. The scalar product of two vectors is the product of their intensities multiplied by the cosine of the angle α between them:

$$\vec{d} \cdot \vec{D} = |\vec{d}| \times |\vec{D}| \cos \alpha$$

The composition of the two conatus finds its resultant intensity diminished by the drift (since the cosine of an angle is always less than 1), that is, by the misalignment of their respective vectors represented by the angle α (see Figure 1 below). Only the component d_1 of d is 'useful' to the master-vector D. 'Useful' stands here for aligned, namely, striving in the same direction. However, this useful component has an intensity (represented geometrically by its length) –

$$|\vec{d_1}| = |\vec{d}| \cos \alpha$$

– which is inferior to $|\vec{d}|$. The cosine of the angle α is therefore the measure of the loss on account of the imperfect co-linearity of the two conatus-vectors. It follows that a conatus allows itself to be enlisted in proportion to the degree of its co-linearity. When the two efforts are orthogonal, there is a right angle between $\vec{d}$ and $\vec{D}$, the cosine is equal to 0, and the loss is total: the conatus is maximally unruly and leaves nothing to be captured by the master-desire. Conversely, when the angle is 0 the cosine is equal to 1, co-linearity is perfect, and there is full alignment: the enlisted desire lives completely for the master-desire.

FIGURE 1

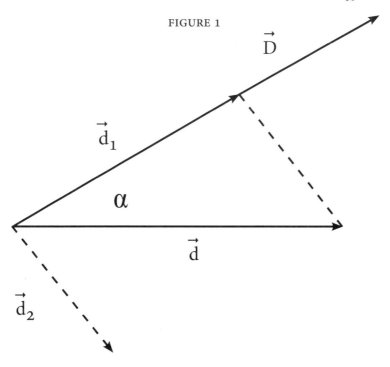

A = 0!

In the multidimensional space of objects of desire, the individual conatus-vectors 'spontaneously'[32] set their own coordinates, that is, the multiple directions in which they strive with specific intensities. From this fact ensues for each an angle α, which, taking into consideration the structural constraints (notably those weighing on material reproduction), indicates its idiosyncratic inclinations (directions) and measures which part of its power of acting can be captured by the boss D, and which part cannot. The angle α is the *clinamen* of the individual conatus, its spontaneous

---

32   The quotation marks signify a linguistic convenience since individuals are not the authors of their desires, which, governed by passive affects, always come to them partially from without. Heteronomy is always the law of the orientation of the conatus-vectors, and 'spontaneity' is determined from outside.

misalignment relative to the ends of the enterprise: α thus expresses the persistent heterogeneity of the conatus relative to the master-desire, and its sine (which corresponds to the orthogonal component d_2) is the measure of that which refuses capture.

Reducing the drift and perfecting the alignment. This is evidently the obsession of the capitalist boss, but in a wider sense also of the boss in general, as it is the very figure of a master-desire, namely, of an enlister, regardless of the nature of the latter's *enterprise* (object of desire). The obsession with alignment is simply the desire to turn the enlisted powers into a faithful extension of one's own power. It is particularly visible in small (capitalist) businesses, where bosses and employees are in daily contact with one another. The bosses (and owners) of such enterprises watch over their employees and conclude that they are not doing enough, or not well enough, or not fast enough – in other words they see themselves in their employees, making them an extension of themselves, almost a surrogate, to whom they directly ascribe their own desires and then fail to understand how these desires could be so poorly served by those they have made in their imagination, by a kind of meta-desire, their *alter egos*. The meta-desire to align the enlistees in the service of one's desire is the meta-desire of the full communication of the (master-)desire, the fantasy of making others identical to oneself. If large enterprises eliminate these occasions for interpersonal contact that contribute so much to the fantasy, not perhaps of fusion, but of the absorption of the enlistees in the enlister, they nonetheless retain something similar in their commonplace edifying maxims – for example, top bosses who claim to be 'as demanding of others as of themselves', thus transmuting the projections of their own desire, made master-desire, into a moral virtue, and expressing in a blind adage of conative egocentricity the wish that others make that desire fully their *own*.

As if the geometry of aligning efforts left a deposit in language, the common usage gets it right when it gives certain master-desires the title of 'directors'. This is indeed what it is about: orienting the conatus-vectors in a certain direction. The spur of hunger and the promise of expanded consumption were the first two mechanisms producing the alignment of the enlisted conatus with the vector of the capitalist boss's conatus. It would seem that neither achieved the goal of perfect co-linearisation, since for the last few decades capitalism has felt the need to 'switch methods'. Let us say immediately that if the method is changing, it is because the ambition has changed. The residual α-s that used to be tolerated have become intolerable. The neoliberal enterprise has reached the conclusion that α is always too large. Its new goal is $\alpha = 0$. Indeed, the formula $\alpha = 0$ corresponds very closely to what increasing research in the sociology of organisations reveals about a goal of *total* mobilisation of individuals in the service of the enterprise.

As a first approximation, one can attribute this desire of total enlistment to two evolutions in the structures of capitalism. The first resides in the transformations in finance that led to the rise of shareholder power[33] and in the competitive deregulation of markets in goods and services, both in synergy altering the balance of forces between capital and labour at the expense of the second, so much so that capital feels authorised to demand *anything* without encountering any significant force capable of dissuading it. To give an idea, almost a *measure*, of this hegemony of shareholder-controlled capital, it is enough to point out the upward drift in its claims on added value over the last few decades, estimated directly from the share of dividends in GDP,[34] or indirectly from the rate of

---

33 On the nature and history of this transformation, see Frédéric Lordon, *La politique du capital*, Odile Jacob, 2002, and *Et la vertu sauvera le monde. Après la crise financière, le salut par 'l'éthique'?* Raisons d'agir, 2003.

34 The share of dividends in France's GDP rose from 3.2 per cent in 1982 to 8.5 per cent in 2007. See Gilbert Cette, Jacques Delpla and Arnaud Sylvain, *Le partage des fruits de la croissance en France*, Rapport du CAE n° 85, La Documentation Française, 2009.

return on net equity that shareholders demand from the biggest companies.[35]

The second of these evolutions relates rather to the transformation of the productive tasks, both the growing emphasis on the relational and attitudinal competences expected of service-sector workers, and the forms of 'creativity' required to sustain the fast-paced innovation that has become the principal weapon of competitive strategies. These new tasks without clear demarcations represent a break relative to the Fordist enterprise, whose well-defined and specific tasks fixed fairly precisely the quantum of the power of acting that needed to be mobilised, and were therefore tolerant of the loss of the 'remainder'. The conjunction of unlimited pressures to raise productivity, particularly those resulting from ever higher targets of financial return, with the relative indeterminacy of tasks, opens the perspective of an unlimited commitment of the self for employees called upon to enter a regime of *total vocation*.[36] Since the neoliberal enterprise, unlike the Fordist factory, does not provide employees with a well-defined list of actions to complete, it turns to moulding the desires and dispositions from which actions spring. Moving up a notch – from actions to the dispositions that generate actions – opens considerably, ideally to infinity, the field of predictable actions, thus gaining a level of flexibility that enterprises claim they must have in order

---

35   This rose from a few percentage points at the beginning of the 1990s to levels regularly exceeding 20 per cent today.

36   On the neoliberal enterprise's project for the total investment of employees, see, among others, Pierre Dardot and Christian Laval, *La nouvelle raison du monde. Essai sur la société néolibérale*, La Découverte, 2009 [translated as *The New Way of the World*, Verso, 2013]; Vincent de Gauléjac, *La société malade de la gestion*, Seuil, 2004; Marie-Anne Dujarier, *L'idéal au travail*, PUF, 2006; Jean-Pierre Durand and Marie-Christine Le Floch (eds), *La question du consentement au travail. De la servitude volontaire à l'implication contrainte*, L'Harmattan, 2006; Geneviève Guilhaume, *L'ère du coaching. Critique d'une violence euphémisée*, Syllepse, 2009.

to survive in an intensely competitive and above all highly unstable environment.

THE INTENSIFICATION OF FEAR

In terms of both quantitative (share of GDP, financial rate of return) and qualitative capture (mobilisation of employees), neoliberal capitalism tips into the delirium of the unlimited. That is because, aside from external regulation through the opposition of countervailing forces, the absence of limits is in fact part of the very concept of the capitalist conatus; in the absence of such forces, economic power [*puissance*] seeks its own unlimited increase. Capital's delirium of the unlimited is therefore firstly a strategic symptom, the index of a certain landscape of forces and notably of the state of the forces of resistance, more precisely of their non-existence. It is thus unremarkable that capitalist conatus push their advantage indefinitely, since only the encounter with a contrary and superior force could persuade them to desist. This landscape of forces is none other than that produced by the structures of the contemporary configuration of capitalism, for the structures and the position of agents within these alone determine the distribution of the resources of power [*pouvoir*] (to speak of power in that sense, although eloquent, is not ideal, since the word gives a substantial connotation to what is entirely a relational effect). It is nevertheless the case that the equilibrium of the capital–labour relation is significantly different in the two configurations of capitalism in which it can be analysed.

In the Fordist configuration, competitive pressures were moderated by trade barriers, relocations were almost impossible because of the system of control of direct investments, shareholder pressure was nearly non-existent (rump stock market, strong takeover protections through networks of cross-ownership, international capital flow controls), and economic policy was geared toward both growth and employment, due to the relative emphasis on internal growth. In the current configuration, the liberalisation of markets of goods and services releases competitive pressures between socio-productive systems with widely different standards; direct investments, also liberalised, freely permit relocations, shareholder pressure is intense, and economic policy is mostly geared to curbing inflation. In the transition from one structural configuration to the next, the balance of power [*puissance*] between capital and labour changed radically, since in the second one labour is faced with the collapse, one by one, of all the barriers that once checked capital's push towards maximum profits. Why would capital fail to make the most of its strategic advantage in the new configuration (to whose shaping it contributed not insignificantly by demanding and obtaining suitable transformations)? As might be expected, so long as it encounters no resistance, capital marches on.

Without being representative, some extreme examples of its advances are nevertheless telling, and say a lot about the permissive attitude that took over, testifying to the intoxication that comes of being able to dare everything that one used to hold back on (and that had yet to be formulated even as an idea). To close a site in France, not because it is in deficit, but because it is 'insufficiently profitable', while paying lip service to the obligation to offer employees the option to relocate – to Hungary or Romania for 300 euros a month – is the kind of gesture that continues to shock public opinion, yet that capital no longer hesitates to permit itself. Infamy is a risk it is willing to take with a light and cynical heart, for it remains powerless – for the time being, anyway. The ease with which capital accepts infamy is a crude expression of a strategic situation skewed in its favour to an outrageous degree. But it also adds a quality of provocation and arrogance, a faithful reflection of the sense – indeed quite accurate – that it has of its own power [*puissance*]. Such egregious cases should not obscure its low-grade everyday domination, notably the intensification of the practices of co-linearisation. Since it is 'made necessary' by external pressures – and indeed since everything is permitted (because of those very pressures) – co-linearisation can abandon its old tolerance for residual deviations and set as its target the perfect alignment of enlisted conatus, at least as the ideal upper limit. Obviously, one part of this over-alignment comes directly from a radicalisation of bosses' governance through fear, which both the structures and the conjuncture of mass unemployment they engender render easier than ever. The constant threats of relocation, redundancies, and, ultimately, loss of employment merely exploit the primal affect of the employment relation, monetary dependence and the fear of losing the conditions necessary for the reproduction of material life; but they raise this affect to levels of intensity not seen for a long time, which allow them to extract from employees – through fear – a supplement of subjection and productive mobilisation in the paradoxical form that Thomas Coutrot calls 'forced cooperation.'[37]

LIQUIDITY, THE FANTASY OF CAPITALIST MASTER-DESIRE

The blackmail of material reproduction, that particular fear affect whose canonical form in the world of employment is the threat of losing one's job, only reached this level of intensity because of a dramatic shift in the norms of the enterprise, a shift in whose wake the lay-off, euphemistically called 'workforce adjustment' or 'social programme' – an expression whose literal meaning should give us pause – became a regular practice of management. There is no such thing as autonomous morality,

---

37 Thomas Coutrot, *L'entreprise néolibérale, nouvelle utopie capitaliste?*, La Découverte, 1998.

and the virtue of agents develops in proximity to the interest they have in virtue: either the virtuous behaviour appears directly profitable,[38] or it does not prove too costly. If the Fordist restraint regarding lay-offs could appear as a moral norm, it was above all, then, because the structures, and the conjunctions of these structures, offered enough stability for the business enterprise to be able to dispense with adjustments through changes in the size of the workforce, making the nice gesture of maintaining full employment very affordable. That this was not the result of any moral intention did not prevent ascribing to this mode of employment the status of a moral norm of sorts, according to which depriving employees of the conditions of their material reproduction was too harsh a measure to be used in purely economic strategic decisions, or worse, to be used deliberately as a lever to manipulate the general balance of power. One must evidently be singularly naive to imagine that the idea of 'showing the door' to those who 'aren't happy' remained foreign to the Fordist bosses, but as the flourishing conditions of the labour market and the ease of finding another job stripped the threat of its dramatic consequences, the fact of economic stability acquired the consistency of a norm: to reduce employees to material destitution was an impossibility, the positive and the normative conflated.

The misunderstanding inherent in this confusion of what is a fact (for some) but is lived as a norm (by others) bursts into broad daylight when economic structures change and the spread of deregulation puts new pressures on businesses, which then turn them into so many strategic opportunities to alter the balance of power between capital and labour. The new 'fact' of the neoliberal transformation and its specific programme of adjustments then comes to mean a breach of the norm: lay-offs are no longer the taboo that they were generally held to be – a

---

38   But, it must be said, the profits are not necessarily monetary.

belief that proved to be risky. The brutality of the blackmail through the threat to material reproduction breaks the old norm – in so far as it could be considered a moral one – and, made regular practice, becomes the new norm. But it is a practical and amoral norm, expressing no more than the naked imbalance of a situation in which some hold all the cards and others none. Capital's power [*pouvoir*] to draw the powers of acting [*puissance*] of employees to its own enterprise, but through the sad affects of fear, represents the liberation of a master-desire that no longer feels restrained by anything and is ready to avail itself of every opportunity to impose its will unilaterally. This kind of tyranny, it bears repeating, has its conditions of possibility in the new state of the economic structures of deregulated capitalism; but its model, one could even say its paradigm, is above all the particular master-desire of *financial* capital in the form of *liquidity*.

Understood as the option to exit an asset market at any moment, an option made possible by the certainty of finding a counterparty (a buyer) and by a volume of activity that assures the absorption of the exit transaction (the sale of titles) by the market without significant price variations, liquidity is a promise of *perfect reversibility* offered to financial investors. It represents the minimal form of committing funds, since, in contrast to investment in industrial capital, where money-capital must be immobilised for a long while, the taking of a stake in the form of holding of financial titles of ownership (stocks) can be instantaneously annulled by a simple sell order that returns the position to *cash*. That is why, indeed, the single word 'liquidity' refers simultaneously both to a property of financial markets and to money itself, as the general equivalent to which the aforementioned property allows one to return at will. Financial liquidity serves then as a paradigm twice: first as access to money, general equivalent and object of the market meta-desire, and second as a model of total reversibility. Keynes had already noted the fundamentally anti-social character of liquidity,[39] as the refusal of any durable commitment and Desire's desire to keep all options permanently open – namely, to *never have to take the other into consideration*. Perfect flexibility – the unilateral affirmation of a desire that engages knowing that it can disengage, that invests with the guarantee of being able to disinvest, and that hires in the knowledge that it can fire (*at whim*) – is the fantasy of an individualism pushed to its ultimate consequences, the imaginative flight of a whole era.

Once limited to asset markets, and to a very specific property of them, the scheme of liquidity irresistibly overflows and spreads throughout the whole of capitalist society, evidently primarily serving those in a position to assert their desire as a master-desire. Even though no market, especially not that of labour, can attain the degree of flexibility-reversibility of financial markets, liquidity draws the bullseye and pushes the master-desires towards obtaining the structural transformations that would allow them to get as close to it as they can. The most typical example of that is the capitalist argument that the only way to lower unemployment is to completely liberate layoffs from any regulatory framework. What is really expressed in this argument is the meta-desire to benefit fully from the institutional conditions that allow for the unrestricted pursuit of desire, a kind of May 1968 for bosses (who constitute perhaps the social group that took that moment the most seriously – they truly 'enjoy without fetters'). This is also the subliminal message of the theory of pure and perfectly competitive markets: everything should be capable of adjusting itself instantaneously. But to what? Adjusting to the vacillations of the master-desires, for this is what characterises the passionate life in an uncertain environment: it fluctuates and is open to

---

39   See in this matter André Orléan, 'L'individu, le marché et l'opinion: réflexions sur le capitalisme financier', *Esprit* (November 2000).

continual reorientations. As the property that allows the incorporation of information in real time and the resulting ability to instantaneously modify the composition of a portfolio, liquidity in the narrow sense (financial liquidity) acquires a broad signification: the unconditional right of desire to do as it pleases.

TYRANNY AND TERROR

In the implicit paradigm of liquidity, the master-desire no longer tolerates restrictions on its strategic moves and embraces the idea of no longer having to take the other into consideration. Laying off *as needed*, for example, must become a 'natural' option – namely, of self-evident legitimacy – just as desire, through the ingrained egocentricity of the conatus, is led to consider all its requisites 'natural', since they are *its* requisites. The master-desires would rather ignore that this claim cannot be universalised, but who cares? The entire structure of contemporary capitalism allows them to indulge it. There is no longer anything to restrain capital's unilateral imposition, not even (especially not) moral or reputational codes, as the joyful outrages to which capital abandons itself testify. The egocentricity of the conatus, when it enjoys a favourable power asymmetry, necessarily leads to abuse. For this is not an isolated desire pursuing its objects by its own means, but a master-desire, namely, a desire engaging with powers of acting other than its own, within collaborative relations which it seeks to reshape into relations of subordination. If the structures that organise this hierarchical relation shift the balance of power to the point that it no longer exercises any restraint on the actions of the dominant power, authorising all of its unilateral self-assertions, domination turns into tyranny.

Can it be objected, against the abuse of language that often attaches to this word, that tyranny, namely, the 'desire to dominate beyond one's station',[40] consists in 'wanting to have something in one way when it can only be had in another'[41] – for example, 'I am handsome therefore I must be feared, I am strong therefore I must be loved'[42] – whereas, despotic as it may be, the capitalist master-desire does not exceed its station? That would be to forget that 'unity which does not depend on multiplicity is tyranny' as well.[43] For this 'non-dependence' is evidently not a non-relation; the sovereign-tyrant – the one of 'unity' – remains the boss of the multitude and the capturer of its power. What is meant therefore by this 'non-dependence' is the unilateral imposition of the one's desire upon the multitude, the latter being enlisted without any consideration, subjugated to the whim of a master who is 'independent', thus without limits or any inclination for compromise. Caligula addressed the patricians with 'darling', and made them run in circles around his litter.[44] The taste for ridicule plays no role in the capitalist bosses' desire, which indeed in this perspective does not exceed its station; it always instrumentalises its enlistees in view of the one and only goal of accumulation. Yet the unprecedented degree to which it pushes the ignorance of the Kantian maxim of not using others as means to an end, and its aiming for the unlimited subordination of others to the requisites of its own enterprise, are very much the signs of an evolution toward tyranny – according to this definition of 'independent unity'.

The capitalist adoption of the fantasy of liquidity, the quest for the perfect, instantaneous adjustment of others to one's

40   Blaise Pascal, *Pensées and Other Writings*, trans. Honor Levi, Oxford University Press, 2008, p. 23 (92).
41   Ibid., p. 22 (91).
42   Ibid., p. 23 (91).
43   Ibid., p.121 (501).
44   Albert Camus, *Caligula and Other Plays*, trans. Justin O'Brien, Vintage, 1962.

requisites as master-desire, combines with the endless upward trend in productivity targets to put an unprecedented strain on enlistees, in a context where the backdrop of mass unemployment and the weakening of the strictures on lay-offs render the threat to material reproduction permanent. What the capitalist master-desire in the neoliberal era seeks is nothing less than the liquefaction of labour-power, making the overall size of the workforce into something fluid, reversible, and as easily adjustable as the components of a portfolio of financial assets, with the inevitable effect of creating a world of extreme uncertainty for enlistees. The differential accommodation of economic hazards offers an eloquent condensation of the dramatic shift in the balance of power between capital and labour. Was not capital's claim to a part of the revenues originally justified by its willingness to assume economic risk, with employees abandoning a part of the added value of their labour in exchange for a *fixed* remuneration, shielded from the vagaries of the market? Yet the new structural conditions endow the capitalist desire with enough strategic latitude that it is able to decline to bear even the weight of cyclicality, pushing the task of adjusting to it onto the class of employees, precisely those who were constitutively exempt from it. Against all logic, it is the mass of employees that must from now on adapt to the fluctuations in the level of activity. What room remains for negotiation is now limited to choosing from various forms of adjustment to the market, whether through the deceleration of wage growth, the intensification of efforts, or headcount reductions. This kind of shift provides a measure of the displacement in the power balance and the liberation of a desire that is no longer restrained by anything. Being reduced to passively awaiting the commandments of a master-desire turned tyrannical plunges the class of employees in a world of terror. 'You're looking grumpy. I wonder, can it be because I had your son killed?' Caligula asks Lepidus, who ('choking', note the stage directions) has no choice but to respond, 'Certainly not, Caius. Quite the contrary.'[45] No doubt the neoliberal enterprise is not there yet. Nevertheless, even according to a former executive of a large firm, whom one would rather expect to defend the system that treated him so well, employees go to work every day 'dying of fear.'[46]

---

45   Ibid., Act II, Scene V.
46   Teodor Limann, *Morts de peur. La vie de bureau*, Les empêcheurs de penser en rond, 2007.

CHAPTER TWO

Joyful Auto-Mobiles
(Employees: How to Pull Their Legs)[1]

INTRINSIC JOYFUL EFFECTS

Contradictory as it may sound, tyrants would rather be loved! The task of enlisting powers of acting is a matter of co-linearisation, namely, of the production of suitable desires (suitable to the master-desire). Capitalism must therefore be grasped not only in its structures but also as a certain *regime of desire*; for the pleasure of a Foucauldian derivation, we could call it an *epithumè*.[2] To speak of *epithumè* is another way of recalling that objective structures, as Bourdieu already noted, but also Marx, extend necessarily into subjective structures, and that in addition to being external, social things, they must also exist as inscriptions inside individual psyches. In other terms, social structures find expression as configurations of desires and affects, and thus have their own specific imaginary. To speak of capitalism as *epithumè* is however also to say that, among the multiplicity of social structures, those linked with capitalist relations have acquired a consistency and a centrality that make them the organising principle of the greater part of social life. The capitalist *epithumè* does not exhaust the variety of desires that exist within contemporary societies, but it captures the larger part that is common to them: in these societies, desiring predominantly conforms to the capitalist order of things – or,

---

1 This is a pun: the French expression *faire marcher* means to make someone walk, to make something function, and also to pull someone's leg or lead them on. [Trans.]

2 From the Greek *epithumia*, which means desire.

put otherwise, to manners of desiring under capitalist social relations. In a certain way, therefore, the idea of the *epithumè* as an identifiable regime of desire only has meaning in reference to the coherence of a set of relations and practices. It would be perhaps easier to see its features on a small scale, for example that of the universes Bourdieu describes as 'fields', sites where agents engaged in the same social 'game' converge. Bourdieu uses the term *illusio* for the agents' interests in being caught up in the 'game'. The term *epithumè* applies to similar things, namely, the very forces that drive the engagement in the game, but with the distinctive advantage of indicating how much this 'interest' is in the end, and in keeping with the organic link between interest and conatus, a matter of desire, hence of affects.

The capitalist *epithumè* extends also to the macro-social level. One could even ask whether capitalist society is not the first to exhibit a *comprehensive* regime of desire and affects – here, too, the word 'comprehensive' does not signify exhaustiveness but rather gives a sense of the scale. Another question is how one should qualify the preceding *epithumè*, should it be possible to identify one with comparable properties in scope, consistency, and structuring hold on desiring imaginaries – perhaps the *epithumè* of salvation? The capitalist *epithumè* enumerates the objects of desire that are worthy of pursuit and the affects born from their pursuit, within the scope of the fundamental objectal triptych of money, commodities and labour, to which we can add the supplemental generic object of greatness, hanging above as if to form a tetrahedron but specifically redefined according to the three vertices of the base (the three distinctions of fortune, ostentatiousness, and professional achievements).

The *epithumè* is the product of the incessant work that society carries out on itself. But it is also the product of the incessant work of agents or groups of agents within it who are interested in promoting imaginaries of desire that better align with their own particular plans. One can use the word 'epithu-mogenesis' to name this second type of desire-producing work, a deliberate engineering of affects that is not always left to the great 'process without a subject' that constitutes the social body's self-affections, but is at times steered toward very specific ends, as testified by the active investment of the neoliberal enterprise in practices of co-linearisation.

Of course, everything said before about monetary dependence and its hierarchical refraction inside the organisation, or about the attachment to the commodity through consumption, is already fully within the scope of a discussion of the capitalist *epithumè*: are not the money that ensures survival and the objects whose accumulation makes us rejoice matters of desire and affect? But in manifesting as never before the intention of achieving zero α, the recent transformations of the employment relation help clarify that, precisely in what concerns employment, the capitalist *epithumè* does not end there. The passionate temperament of employment, now richer than both the Marxian thesis of naked exploitation and its continuation in the sociology of Fordist consumption implicitly assumed, ends neither with the desire for the money that affords survival, nor with that for the consumption goods that solicit the compulsion to buy.

But in what exactly does this extension of the passionate temperament of employment, required by the neoliberal quest for full alignment, consist? Necessarily, in enrichment in joyful affects; or more precisely, in the production of *intrinsic* joyful affects. The first enrichment – that which gave the capitalist *epithumè* its Fordist configuration – consisted in supplementing the sad affects of the spur of hunger with the joyful affects of the expanded access to consumable commodities, augmenting the desire to avoid an evil (material destitution) with the desire to pursue goods (but only in the form of amassable, material goods). No doubt this first addition did much to motivate employees to align themselves with the master-desire of capital. But the neoliberal enterprise has nonetheless found this to be insufficient. From now on it would take upon itself to do the epithumogenic work directly.

And this is its specific strategic contribution: the spur of hunger was intrinsic to employment, but it was a sad affect. Consumerist joy is indeed a joyful affect, but it is an extrinsic one. The neoliberal epithumogenesis undertakes to produce *intrinsic joyful affects*, that is, affects that are intransitive rather than ceded to objects outside the activity of wage labour itself (as consumption goods are). Hence it is the activity *itself* that must be reconstructed, both objectively and in the imagination, as a source of *immediate* joy. The desire to find employment should no longer be merely a mediated desire for the goods that wages *circuitously* permit buying, but an intrinsic desire for the activity for its own sake. Neoliberal epithumogenesis thus assumes the specific task of producing on a large scale desires that did not previously exist, or that existed only in a minority of capitalist enclaves: desires for happy labour, or, to borrow directly from its own vocabulary, desires for 'fulfilment' and 'self-realisation' in and through work. And the fact is that, at least instrumentally, it gets it right. Intrinsically sad or extrinsically joyful, the affects-desires that capitalism was proposing to its enlistees fell short of taking away the sting of the idea that 'real life is elsewhere'; in other words, they did not eliminate the residual α-s. But what if it can now convince employees that their working life would more and more become simply their life, and that the former would provide the latter with its best opportunities for joy? Would any supplemental mobilisation be too much to expect? For employees used to surrender to the master-desire with a heavy heart, or while contemplating external joys in which the latter's plans played no role. To cut a long story short, they had other things on their minds. But if their attitude changes from reluctance to 'consent', they will be moved differently. Differently means more intensely.

THE APORIAE OF CONSENT

Ideally, the present-day enterprise would like clockwork-orange employees: subjects who strive of their own accord according to its norms. Being (neo)liberal, it would like them to be free in addition to being mechanical: mechanical for the functional certitude, and free both for the sake of ideological beauty and because it considers that relying on free will is ultimately the surest way to obtain *unreserved* action from employees, that is, the surrender of their power of acting in full. The extreme nature of both the vision of the neoliberal enterprise and its processes eloquently testifies to the enrichment of the passionate economy of the employment relation that it hopes to use, not unjustifiably, as its support. For the bottom line is that, indeed, employees increasingly function by themselves. Without wishing to play too much on words, we can say that the clockwork-oranges are 'auto-mobiles'. If auto-mobility is the quality of that which moves itself, then the production of employed auto-mobiles – namely, employees who occupy themselves of their own accord in the service of the capitalist organisation – is incontestably the greatest success of the neoliberal co-linearisation undertaking. For the first and most patent meaning of the expression 'of their own accord' is 'in the absence of any pressure', without being forced, by their own movement. The sociology (or social psychology) of work is indeed full of references to this fact (a strange one, relative to the atmosphere of coercion that used to surround work), this new 'voluntary servitude' whose mechanisms it would like to study, this form of servitude that is obviously special, since, in fact, the enslaved *consent* to it.

But this question that the social sciences of labour rediscover for themselves is as old as political philosophy. For

consent is one of those notions, like obedience and legitimacy, and, conversely, compulsion and coercion, that surround the mystery of power [*pouvoir*] as 'action on actions',[3] as the art of *making others do something*. Is this really so mysterious to the modern understanding? Less and less, it seems, judging by the immediacy with which the idea of 'consent' appears to be grasped. But this straightforwardness is deceptive, or rather, the truth that it speaks is about something else, not the idea of consent itself, but rather its relation with a certain intellectual configuration within which it assumes its self-evident character. That configuration is not recent, but it is ours more than ever. For the false transparency of consent is a symptom of the metaphysics of subjectivity, and the difficulties of the one are immediately those of the other as well.

Yet everything seems to begin with the greatest ease: consent is the intimate approbation given by a free will. When consent is voiced, it is the solid core of the authentic self that speaks. There is an autonomous ego, whose existence is not in doubt, which, under appropriate conditions, manifests itself as both the origin and the norm of giving consent. It seems therefore that we have a good grasp of what consent is; yet there is no shortage of problematic instances. The 'this is my choice' that should end discussion, since there is nothing prior to the founding and self-founded subject, is incapable of quelling all doubts; there are individual instances of consent to which outside observers refuse to give their consent. For example: he follows a guru but nobody forced him to; she wears the veil but it was her decision; s/he shuts her/himself away in the office for twelve hours a day, but purely out of personal choice, uncompelled by anyone – unexplainable embarrassments in which the intellectual

---

3   Michel Foucault, 'The Subject and Power', in Hubert L. Dreyfus and Paul Rabinow, *Michel Foucault: Beyond Structuralism and Hermeneutics*, Harvester Press, 1982.

and practical ethos of subjectivity should in principle find nothing to fault. The contradiction these instances expose between the refusal to validate the consent and the orthodox form it takes – since in all these cases it is expressed in the first person, and by subjects explicitly articulating their sincerity and the absence of compulsion – cannot easily be resolved, finally leaving only two possible reductions (in fact both are necessary simultaneously): one can argue either, from the side of the objects, that there are things to which it is 'intrinsically' impossible to consent, or, from the side of the subjects, that their consent was falsely or fraudulently obtained. But does not then the fact of experiencing such lapses call into question their very quality as subjects? And, following that, how does one determine when a subject is fit *qua* subject and when not?

The Spinozist point of view cuts radically through these difficulties. For if the act of giving consent is the authentic expression of a freely self-determined interiority, then consent does not exist. If it is understood as the unconditioned approbation of a subject that proceeds only from itself, then it does not exist, for heteronomy is the condition of all things, including all human things, and no action is such that anyone could claim it entirely as his or hers. All things are in the grip of inadequate causation; namely, they are partially determined to act by other, external things.[4] The individualistic ethos, which is the continuation of the metaphysics of subjectivity, refuses to the last to consider such an idea. True, at stake is nothing less than its outright dissolution, and a habit of thinking and relating to oneself that is by now so entrenched will not easily give way. Except by the violence of a kind of conversion, the idea of

---

4   'I call that cause adequate whose effect can be clearly and distinctly perceived through it. But I call it partial, *or* inadequate, if its effect cannot be understood through it alone.' *Ethics*, III, Definition 1. 'I say that we are acted on when something happens in us, or something follows from our nature, of which we are only a partial cause.' *Ethics*, III, Definition 2.

full determination cannot readily defeat the deeply ingrained belief in the faculty of self-determination on which individuals rest their identities as 'subjects'. Yet, with supreme deftness, as if to cap the destabilisation of this belief and to emphasise precisely that it is merely a belief, Spinoza discloses the genetic principle of this idea, that is, the mechanism of its begetting in the imagination: 'men are deceived in thinking themselves free, a belief that consists only in this, that they are conscious of their actions and ignorant of the causes by which they are determined'.[5] The idea of their freedom is merely the effect of a deficient capacity of intellection and the truncation that results from it. Incapable, for obvious reasons, of tracing back the infinite chain of antecedent causes, they record only their volitions and their actions, and take the shortest path, which consists in considering themselves their true source and only origin. But no action is more than a moment in the infinite sequence of the determination of things by things. 'Any thing which is finite and has a determinate existence, can neither exist nor be determined to produce an effect unless it is determined to exist and produce an effect by another cause, which is also finite and has a determinate existence,' states the *Ethics* with geometrical austerity, a manner of saying that we only do something when something happens to us.[6]

This is indeed the meaning of the elementary sequence affection-affect-action – we are very tempted to contract it into *affectaction* – which calls for the entreaty of a prior encounter,

---

5   Ibid., II, 35, Scholium.
6   Ibid., I, 28: 'Every singular thing, or any thing which is finite and has a determinate existence, can neither exist nor be determined to produce an effect unless it is determined to exist and produce an effect by another cause, which is also finite and has a determinate existence; and again, this cause also can neither exist nor be determined to produce an effect unless it is determined to exist and produce an effect by another, which is also finite and has a determinate existence, and so on, to infinity.'

an 'ad-venture' – that which happens [*advient*] to us, as Barthes reminds us[7] – in order to make the free energy of the conatus attach itself to something, an object or a plan, and in *conse-quence* engage in a precise and determinate action. Because it is *our* energy, the energy of our conatus, which occupies itself in the desiring mobilisation, we may say that it is *our* action, and that in that – weak – sense, we act *of our own accord*, we are auto-mobile. But this '*of our own accord*' merely an actantial indication; it has nothing to say about everything that preceded it. And although we are auto-mobiles, we are irremediably hetero-determined. No doubt our force of desire, our power of acting, fully belongs to us. But it owes everything to the inter-pellations of things, namely, to external encounters, when the issue is knowing the path and the direction it takes.

The question of the authenticity or the ownership of desire vanishes once the subjectivist point of view is abandoned and attention is turned outside, to the infinite concatenation of causes, since it is equally true that, being exogenously deter-mined, none of my desires is of my doing, and that as the very expression of my conative force, each of my desires is indisput-ably mine. And this is where the idea of consent begins to founder, shipwrecked together with its opposite, alienation. For if to be alienated is to be prevented from proceeding from oneself and to find oneself instead chained to an 'other than oneself', then alienation is merely another word for hetero-determination, namely, for passionate servitude, the human condition itself (governed by passive affects). If alienation is determination by the outside, nothing is outside alienation, since nothing 'which is finite and has a determinate existence, can either exist or be determined to produce an effect unless it is determined to exist and produce an effect by another cause,

---

7 Roland Barthes, *Camera Lucida: Reflections on Photography*, Hill and Wang, 1981, reprint 2010.

which is also finite, etc.' Thus, to the real etymology of alienation, which declares the presence of something other than the
self (*alien*, *alius*) within self-direction, we can add an imaginary
etymology, one which would rather hear in 'alienate' the word
'lien', tie, thus rediscovering in it the infinite chain of the production of effects within which we are both caused and causing. If,
understood thus, to be alienated is to be chained, then far from
applying only to exceptional attachments – and such that we are
unable to say objectively what is exceptional about them (apart
from not wishing it for ourselves) – alienation is our most ordinary condition, and our most inexorable one. Alienation is thus
another one of the things that do not exist, but in the paradoxical form of an excess of existence: being universal, it is everywhere, and if it does not exist, it is as the obverse of an (unreach-
able) state of wholeness and perfect self-coincidence of the
subject.

The concepts of alienation and 'authentic' consent vanish
therefore together, leaving nothing but the movements of desire,
all equal *under the relation of exo-determination*. With that, the
mania for distinctions and passing judgment has the rug pulled
from underneath it, and it would be hard to deny the discomfort
that ensues at first. For Spinoza goes very far in the renunciation
of classifying people, at least using this criterion alone: 'a man . . .
if he sees that he can live more conveniently on the gallows than
sitting at his own table, would act most foolishly, if he did not
hang himself.'[8] No doubt such a desire would be strange, but it
would be neither 'better' nor 'less well' determined than any
other, and the natural inclination to deem the consenting devo-
tee of the 'hanged life' alienated to the point of absurdity is
promptly avoided. To the subjectivist incoherence that fails to

---

8 Spinoza, Letter XXXVI (XXIII) to Blyenbergh, in *On the Improvement
of the Understanding, the Ethics, Correspondence*, trans. R. H. M. Elwes, Dover
1995, p. 349.

dispel the suspicion of alienation against what are nevertheless instances of formally expressed consent, Spinoza responds with the most extreme consequence: 'But now I let everyone go his own way. Those who wish can by all means die for their own good, provided that I am allowed to live for truth.'[9]

One could go on at length about the implicit politics of this acceptance, the possibility of coexistence between all these different temperaments encapsulated in its entirety in the reservation of the 'provided that', but it is more important in this context to take note of the judgment that Spinoza defuses. As was the case before with the fiction of the free will, and because there is no better way to free oneself from an illusion than by showing how it was created in the imagination, Spinoza reveals the secret behind this stubborn refusal to consent to the consents of others when we do not like them, and the ensuing mania of looking for flaws: 'This striving [conatus] to bring about that everyone should approve of his love and hate is really ambition. And so we see that each of us, by his nature, wants the others to live according to his temperament.'[10] The immense political reach of this statement is obvious; it delivers the principle of all wars of religion and all clashes of civilisation, confrontations between ways of life anxious to be shared and thus validated – because only their imitation by others, think the anxious, could affirm their validity. But, most importantly, Spinoza reveals here the origins of the verdict that certain people are alienated, situating in our own affects – in the loves and hatreds that make us value certain things and not others[11]

---

9   Spinoza, Letter 30 to Oldenburg, in *The Letters*, trans. Samuel Shirley, Hackett, 1995, p. 185.

10   *Ethics*, III, 31, Scholium.

11   'By good here I understand every kind of joy, and whatever leads to it, and especially what satisfies any kind of longing, whatever that may be. And by evil [I understand here] every kind of sadness, and especially what frustrates longing.' *Ethics*, III, 39, Scholium.

– the plenitude of the consent that we accord those who live in conformity with our own temperament, and that we refuse others.

JOYFUL OBEDIENCE

In relation to determination, heteronomy, and passionate servitude, all desires are equal. But other differences remain, for the determination to act that guides the conatus in a specific direction can have a variety of affective moods, which the passionate situation of the employment relation is rich enough to encompass. If common sense resists the idea of including in the category of 'desire' the satisfaction of mere material reproduction, experienced as coercion rather than as a surge of enthusiasm or transport, it is because it pertinently but confusedly makes the distinction between a desire to avoid an evil and a desire to pursue a good. It makes it all the better when, as the common sense of Fordist employment, it clearly sees the difference between the respective affects produced by the daily drudgery of 'making a living' and the joyful prospect of access to consumption goods. However, market objects contribute only a 'transitive' component to the totality of the employees' desire – it is clear at this stage that this desire as a whole is an agglomerate of a plurality of basic desires. The strength of the neoliberal form of the employment relation lies precisely in the re-internalisation of the objects of desire, not merely as desire for money but as desire for other things, for new, intransitive satisfactions, satisfactions inherent in the work activities themselves. Put otherwise, neoliberal employment aims at enchantment and rejoicing: it sets out to enrich the relation with joyful affects.

Employees are under the rule of the enterprise and its commands the way citizens are under the rule of the state and its laws. How people remain loyal to a sovereign entity and to its norms is a question of political philosophy; through what combination of desires and affects they do so is a question of Spinozist political philosophy. It is indeed here that the latter shows its extraordinary generality. Originally a philosophy of powers [*pouvoirs*] and norms identified as political in the narrow sense (powers of the commonwealth and of its government), it reveals itself to be in fact a philosophy of powers and norms of all kinds, found in all social institution.[12] This generality follows a second, much more important one, which can be expressed in a syllogism of sorts: power, especially viewed as Foucault understood it, as conduct of conducts or action on actions, is an *art of making others do things*. But making others do things is precisely the effect of the affects, since an affect is something an affection (an encounter with something) does to me (causing joy or sadness), and *consequently what it makes me do* – for the result of an affect is a redirection of the conatus and the desire to do something. Thus power is in its very mode of operation a matter of producing affects and inducing through affects. Conducting conducts is therefore nothing other than a certain art of affecting, and to govern is indeed, in keeping with etymology, a matter of directing, but in the most literal, even geometrical, sense of the term, namely, a matter of orienting the conatus-vectors of desire in certain directions. Power is the totality of practices of co-linearisation.

Spinoza calls *obsequium* the complex of affects that makes subjected bodies move towards the objects of the norm, namely, that makes subjects – understood here in the sense of *subditus*, not *subjectum*, the subject *of* the sovereign rather than the sovereign subject – do the actions that conform to the requisites of the perseverance of the sovereign's rule. The *obsequium* has

---

12   For a reading of the *Political Treatise* as a general theory of social institutions, see Frédéric Lordon, 'L'empire des institutions', *Revue de la Régulation* 7 (2010), regulation.revues.org; 'La puissance des institutions', *Revue du MAUSS permanente* (April 2010), journal-dumauss.net.

two pure formulae which give rise to the norm-governed orientation of the behaviour whereby the subject follows (*sequor*) the
rule: the 'subjects are so far dependent not on themselves, but
on the commonwealth, as they fear its power or threats, or as
they love the civil state'.[13] Here is then power's bipolar affective
truth: it functions through fear or through love. This truth holds
for all powers, including the bosses' power. And like all powers,
the bosses' power discovers through experience that it is more
 efficient to rule with love than with fear, for people aspire to live
a life worthy of that name: 'I understand a human life, defined
 not by mere circulation of the blood, and other qualities
common to all animals'.[14] But a life reduced to the material
reproduction of bare life offers little beyond the 'circulation of
blood', and no matter how imperiously desirable, does not offer
a horizon for the deployment of the power of acting. Gladdening
the hearts of the subjected is that strategy of power that organises this deployment, but in 'suitable' directions, those of its
own master-desire, ready to be captured. This is how the mobi-
liser undertakes to do away with the 'reserve' of the mobilised,
since the subjected rejoice when they are offered desires they
mistake for their own, and which in fact become their own. It is
then that they set themselves in motion without reserve, and
enter the sweetened universe of consent, whose real name is
happy obedience.

Obedience is nevertheless a burden, for, as Spinoza recalls,
people do not like to be subordinate to those they consider their

---

13   Spinoza, *Political Treatise*, trans. A. H. Gosset, G. Bell & Son, 1883, III, 8.
14   Ibid., V, 5. The reference to blood circulation here is in all likelihood
polemic, directed against Hobbes, for whom political institutions are an additional means for the individual conatus to defend themselves, but who defines the
conatus as the reflex movements of the living body aimed at preserving the vital
function of blood circulation, therefore with an end of mere self-conservation. In
contrast, Spinoza conceives the conatus as movement for the *perseverance in
being* (and not in a given state); thus, tendentiously, as the widest and most varied
realizations of power possible.

equals. Modern individualism rendered obsolete the symbolic strategies of the past, in which the king was endowed with divine attributes that gave him the air of possessing an absolute difference. In a regime based on formal equality, bosses (of all kinds – the enlisters) need other methods of co-linearisation if they are to produce obedience without burden. With or without burden, namely, with sadness or with joy: this is the true antinomy in which the false antinomy of coercion and consent is resolved. The only way to escape the aporiae of consent by some that appears as coercion to others (but in the intermediate form of alienation, since the 'coerced', visibly foreign to themselves, stupidly say 'yes'), is to first take note of universal passionate servitude, in order to *then* entrust the task of making the distinction to its particular affective contents. For although we are all equally enslaved to our passions and chained to our desires, to be happy with one's chains is evidently not the same as to be saddened by them. 'Coercion' and 'consent' are simply the names that the respective affects of sadness and of joy assume inside institutional situations of power and normalisation. This question of naming is however decisive for Spinoza, precisely because of the dead ends that result from allowing words such as coercion and consent to transform simple subjective expressions of affects into objective operations. If Spinoza goes to such lengths to rename everything, and in particular the affects,[15] frustrating lexical habits and at the risk of being poorly understood, it is in order not to fall into the traps created by words belonging to knowledge of the first type, knowledge 'by vague experience', intuitively formed in the proximity of the affects and in ignorance of true causes. As François Zourabichvili notes, Spinoza finds it necessary to invent a new

---

15   'I know that in their common usage these words mean something else. But my purpose is to explain the nature of things, not the meaning of words.' *Ethics*, III, Definitions of the Affects XX, Explication.

language;[16] there is a 'Spinoza-speak'[17] because renaming everything marks the break between knowledge of the first type and
knowledge of the second type, the knowledge of things from
the standpoint of genetic objectivity. Even Durkheim falls in
this trap, for example when he asserts on numerous occasions
that 'coercion' is the *modus operandi* of institutional norms. Yet
'coercion' is simply an emotive term that expresses (subjec-
tively) the objective fact of causal determination, and in that
sense one is no less 'coerced' – in fact, determined – when one
consents. Coercion and consent are forms of the lived experience (respectively sad and joyful) of determination. To be
coerced is to have been determined to do something but in a
state of sadness. And to consent – to consent to follow, in the
sense of the *sequor* of the *obsequium* – is to live one's obedience,
but with its intrinsic burden relieved by a joyful affect.

SPONTANEOUS RE-ENCHANTMENT

Whence come the affects responsible for the happy determination of the *sequor* and for reducing the burden of obedience?
Curiously enough, they come first from the employees themselves, whose own passionate mechanisms of adaptation can
sometimes push them to recolour their situation as enlistees.

What makes this transfiguration possible is the fact that, as
such, no situation or thing imposes a value or a meaning that it
objectively possesses. Spinoza is very insistent on this point.
Value and meaning do not reside in things but are *produced* by
the desiring forces that seize them: 'We neither strive, nor will,
neither want, nor desire anything because we judge it to be
good; on the contrary, we judge something to be good because

---

16   Ibid., IV, 40, Scholium II.
17   François Zourabichvili, *Spinoza, une physique de la pensée*, PUF, 2002.

we strive for it, will it, want it, and desire it.'[18] This statement certainly exemplifies the unsettling strangeness of Spinozist thought and its power to confound our most solid habits of thought, since, in inverting the connection between desire and value, it ruins any possibility of an objectivism of value. Value is not an intrinsic property of things, to which desire, as mere acknowledgment, must simply conform; conversely, our desire is not a simple effort of orientation in a world of desirables that are objectively already there. In perfect opposition to the intuitive representation that posits the anteriority of value to desire, the Scholium of *Ethics*, III, 9 states that, fundamentally, it is in desire's own investments that the valorisation of things originates. Far from desire being induced by value, it is value that is produced by desire. And we are therefore justified in saying that desire is an *axiogenic* power.

Does this mean that situations and things appear before us concretely in a kind of neutral virginity, awaiting our free, axiogenic investment? Obviously not. In each person, the valorisation of things, the spontaneous creative activity of the conatus, is structured under the influence of a set of axiological schemes and already constituted valorisations, into which newly encountered things must find their place along connecting chains that are more or less modulated by the characteristics of the 'encounter situation': exposed to this work of art, I attach to it this value because I can relate it to works of art that I have encountered previously and already valorised; moreover, I encounter it in this place (a museum, a gallery) that I have already recognised as a legitimate institution, and in the company of this person whom I likewise consider an authority in the subject and who praised it before me (or to the contrary, I identify the work of art as unlike those I have already valorised as beautiful, in a place that I consider a priori likely to disappoint me, and taking

18   *Ethics*, III, 9, Scholium.

into consideration favourable opinions, but that were given to me by persons I hold in disfavour). That my valorising (axiogenic) temperament develops over time, and is made richer with every new encounter with things, does not preclude it from having its lines of force and its durable patterns – and this holds even if my temperament can suffer profound and sudden modifications as a result of an extraordinary encounter (one outside my ordinary context). The situation in which a thing encountered for the first time is valorised is not characterised *in practice* – this 'in practice' stands opposed to the 'as such' with which the statement of *Ethics*, III, 9, was introduced – by any axiological isotropy: it does not possess the indifference of a virgin terrain, where all future valorisations are equally probable. My axiological temperament, socially and biographically constituted, exerts therefore a very strong predetermining effect. But neither does it entirely saturate the result, leaving sometimes room for a work of revalorisation that reflects the impact of new passionate necessities.

The employment situation, namely, the encounter with the imposed task, enters the enlistee's valorising temperament, by the very fact that it is a situation of imposition, most probably as a painful and saddening thing, at least for as long as its sole motivation is the desire to avoid the evil of material destitution. But the *vis existendi* of the conatus, which is spontaneously an effort toward joy since joy is an increase in the power of acting, is sometimes capable of reinvesting situations that are at first doomed to be experienced as saddening. 'We strive to further the occurrence of whatever we imagine will lead to joy,' recalls *Ethics*, III, 28. Likewise *Ethics*, III, 12: 'the mind as far as it can, strives to imagine those things that increase or aid the body's power of acting', or, inversely, 'avoids imagining those things that diminish or restrain its or the body's power' (*Ethics*, III, 13, Corollary). As far as it can by its own power, the conatus seeks its joy. It seeks it even in situations that are prima facie the most unfavourable to it: the ultimate example is that Elias, brute and extraordinary force of nature, whose path Primo Levi crossed in the Auschwitz camp, describing him as someone who not only had found his joy but also 'was probably a happy person.'[19]

Whether consciously or not, the general boss (the enlister) capitalises on this propensity. That is why even the most basic jobs, under certain personal and social conditions, sometimes provide room for joyful reinvestment, in which the generic desire produces in a way its own opportunities for specific actualisations by itself, in this case as work that is seen as 'interesting' or meaningful. The indifference to content that Marxist critique identified in the production for exchange value and in undifferentiated, 'abstract labour' is evidently a very strong tendency. But it is not entirely irresistible.

It is not irresistible from the side of capital, whose very process of accumulation and intransitive valuation could doom it to a complete disinterest in substance, leaving it with only the generic interest in the extraction of monetary value. However, despite the sectoral indifference that favours the indiscriminate allocation of money-capital to this activity or that, solely according to the anticipated rate of surplus value, the captains of industrial capital *also* manifest forms of passionate attachment to their particular activity. Of course, this attachment has nothing exclusive about it and can fail to forestall disinvestment and the transfer of capital towards other uses. But neither can it be fully dismissed. Through the moral valorisation of their specific activity, industrial capital(ists) produce(s) forms of vocational identities that are intrinsically tied to content: the identity of the 'builder' for big civil engineering outfits, of the 'historical agent of technological progress' for information technology firms, of the 'lifestyle revolutionary' for the integrated media or

19   Primo Levi, *Survival at Auschwitz*, Touchstone, 1995, p. 98.

telecommunication groups, etc. These productions of meaning and value derive from a desire that is not fully reducible to the desire for monetary accumulation, an extra-monetary desire, which, if it does not always exist beforehand, can arise in the contact with the activity.

Conversely, because it is removed from the concrete appreciation of capital, the conatus of financial capital has contact with absolutely nothing beyond the surplus value that flows back to it. It can therefore form no other desire. It is all the less capable of that since every structure that governs its flow favours this detachment from substance, from the models of portfolio management – which recommend asset diversification through an increased number of small participations in the enterprises of industrial capital – to the structures of liquidity, which lead investors to very frequent round-trips in and out of the capital of those enterprises, which they enter and exit following the winds of differentially anticipated returns and without a second's consideration for the substance of the activities involved. The industrial conatus, which is by its nature invested – in all senses of the terms – in the concreteness of an activity, almost necessarily forms the extra-monetary significations and valorisations of its investments: one can say that it is partial to its activity *as such*. As ridiculous as one may find them, corporate 'identities' and 'cultures' draw on this passionate source and can at times be more than just managerial fabrications. They can correspond to meanings that are authentically experienced, at least by upper management.

Evidently more problematically, these resignifications of an activity formally subservient to exchange value can also take place on the side of the employees. As if the deployment of their very life force simply refused to sink into the sadness of undifferentiated labour, or of meaninglessness, individuals resist the estrangement of a production entirely governed by the abstraction of capital whenever they can: 'the mind as far as it can, strives to imagine those things that increase or aid its power of acting' investing in the contents of the activity in order to discover something desirable in it, and to find opportunities for joy. No doubt it can only do so to a very variable degree, due as much to individual dispositions as to the nature of the specific contents, or rather to the minimal (social) valorisations of which these contents are already the object, and that offer a lever to the imaginary production of the desirable. Whether through a formal ethics of 'a job well done', or through the reinvention of an interest in the substance of the tasks (reinventions experienced as objective discoveries even though they are produced by the individuals themselves), these small transfigurations, when they can take place, help keep the dereliction of abstract labour in check (in the sense used by Marx).

This threat of dereliction in the service of a foreign desire, the threat of the expenditure of the power of acting as pure loss – though obviously the 'loss' is never pure, if only because at the very least the expenditure brings in a salary – can be countered in the end in a very limited number of ways, in fact in only two. One can admit it to oneself, with the consequence of having to choose between resignation (real life is elsewhere, in the other eight waking hours), or even the depression captured by the expression 'a life wasted making a living', and, the antagonistic option, rebellion and struggle (the trade union on the inside, politics on the outside): 'the greater the sadness, the greater is the part of a man's power of acting to which it is necessarily opposed.'[20] Alternatively, unable to face the too painful fact of one's dereliction, the subject strives to 'imagine those things that increase or aid one's power of acting', thus repelling the spectre of sad dejection with the arms of re-enchantment, namely, by recreating a desire of one's own, aligned with the master-desire yet distinct from it. This enables the recuperation

---

20   *Ethics*, III, 37, Demonstration.

of an idiosyncratic meaning that can overcome the void of abstract labour; an object-desire is reconstructed under the effect of a meta-desire for living happily, or at least with joy, or at any rate not meaninglessly. Thus re-concretised and newly charged with desirability, albeit through the very effort of the meta-desire for joyful life, abstract labour can be minimally reappropriated. And so we see employees finding an interest, and subsequently satisfaction, in tasks that they would in all probability deem profoundly uninteresting were they freed from material necessity.

THE LOVE OF THE MASTER

But the primary source for the co-linearising affects of the wage-labour *obsequium* is found externally to the subject, for example, in a localised love – a joy affect accompanied by the idea of an external cause.[21] I obey the master because the master is the imagined (or the real) cause of the blessings that I love and that affect me with joy. I obey the master notably because 'we shall strive to do also whatever we imagine men to look on with joy'[22] – therefore also what a particular individual looks on with joy – and because 'if someone has done something which he imagines affects others with joy, he will be affected with joy accompanied by the idea of himself as cause.'[23] One must not underestimate the generality of this figure of the master, whose particular inflections can be as varied as the guru, the parent, the university professor, the boss, the military commander, the beloved, or even public opinion as the gathering of all – in short, all individuals or groups from whose love a primary joyful affect can be anticipated, together with a secondary one of loving

---

21   Ibid., III, 13, Scholium.
22   Ibid., III, 29.
23   Ibid., III, 30.

oneself through contemplating one's capacity to bring them joy: I do what allows me to please the master, and therefore to be identified by the master as the cause of his or her joy, so that the master will love me and I will take pleasure in having brought joy to the master.

That we immediately recognise this passionate mechanism is not enough to turn it for Spinoza into a simple psychological intuition; in the *Ethics*, the entire interplay of affects is methodically generated according to 'the demonstrative order' (the statements of the *Ethics* are precisely called propositions). But even aside from this apodictic derivation, the relative simplicity of the mechanism gives it a remarkable generative power, to judge by the variety and the 'weight' of the passionate facts to which it provides access: neither more nor less than all the forms of attachment, individual or social, based on the desire for recognition, and all the variants of the search for love. Indeed, the transformation of employment, with the replacement of the demand for monetary compensation by a demand of recognition for commitment and accomplishments, is today one of the most hackneyed questions of the sociology of work. And rightly so, for the displacement of the sentiment of injustice towards issues that can be called symbolic is very real, testifying to the enlargement of the range of satisfactions that work is expected to offer. We no longer work merely to earn money and avoid material destitution; we seek the joy that comes from the joy of those to whom we offer our labour, namely their love.

In keeping with the spirit of the reform of words undertaken by Spinoza, we must not allow ourselves to be confused by the use of the word love to describe situations, such as work and employment, that seem lexically incongruous with it. For once the word love is divorced from our intuitive affective understanding and used according to the requirements of the genetic definition, namely, as simply referring to joy accompanied by the idea of an external cause, then it becomes the most

general term for objectal satisfaction, and therefore capable of
encompassing the full range of possible objects of satisfaction,
from the most modest to the most social, in any case, well
beyond erotic love. That is why Laurent Bove is entirely correct
to speak at the most general level of 'the amorous structure of
behaviour',[24] and to emphasise the fundamentally amorous
nature of desire, whatever its objects happen to be. For the
conatus as power is effort toward more power, namely, the
search for affects of joy, defined by Spinoza precisely as the
augmentation of the body's power of acting,[25] and the avoid-
ance of affects of sadness. That is also why there is no need to
pass through an ontogenetic hypothesis in order to account for
demands for love addressed within social universes such as
employment, by treating them as a metamorphosis (by subli-
mation) of the fundamental demand for love (we are tempted to
capitalise 'Fundamental', in order to signal the absolute primacy
that psychoanalysis accords it) that forms the original bond
between child and parents. The completely general mechanism
of the demand for love is inscribed at the very heart of the conatus as force of desire and as striving towards joyful satisfaction,
and especially in the identification of our capacity to please
others in order to derive joy from being loved by them (*Ethics*,
III, 29, 30). As parents are merely the first point of application
of this basic passionate scheme, parental love cannot claim any
essential psychogenetic primacy, but only a simple chronological precedence;[26] subsequently the demand for love is reactivated as it diversifies in each new encounter with a situation
suitable for offering it new opportunities.

---

24   Laurent Bove, *La stratégie du conatus. Affirmation et résistance chez
Spinoza*, Vrin, 1996, p. 41.
25   *Ethics*, III, Definition 3.
26   Of course, this chronological anteriority is the root of such strong associations that they may lead eventually, as they are reactivated, to carrying the
parental figures into later love quests.

Employment socialisation is evidently one such situation. Among the many objects of desire simultaneously pursued by the overzealous, the conscientious, and the obsequious (the aptly named paragon of the *obsequium*), one finds not only strategic interests such as seeking promotion, receiving a raise, or beating competitors, but also the pursuit of the joy stemming from being loved by a superior, that is, loved both by a particular individual and by the institution (a great amorous power) through one of its representatives. The mechanism of the amorous search for recognition is one of absolute generality, and therefore lends itself to a specific inflection within the world of work. However, the amorous intensity of the employment relation varies according to contingent conditions that determine the wider or narrower latitude available for its expression – one example of widening latitude is the increasingly individualised management of 'human resources', which could be ascribed more generally to the contemporary tendency towards 'psychologising' social relations, and so on. In any case, the love of the boss-master, in the form of the search for recognition, has its rightful place in the passionate complex of employment as one of the forms of its specific 'alienation' – that is, as 'consent', since this love is a source of joyous affects. But by the same token it is also a source of co-linearisation, since, *by its very nature*, the passionate mechanism of the demand for love leads the seeker to do what brings joy to the giver, hence to embrace/anticipate the latter's desire in order to conform one's own to it. As lines of dependence are *also* lines of dependence for recognition, the alignment of the subordinate with the superior, who is already aligned in the same way, is inscribed in the general structure – hierarchical and fractal – of passionate co-linearization.

Thus shaped by both the general structure of the employment relation and its local actualisation in a business enterprise, the general affective mechanisms of the amorous search for recognition have the property of inducing particular conative movements – desires and actions – that contribute 'of themselves' to satisfying the organisation's master-desire (as embodied by its top executives). From the fact that 'the man affected with joy desires nothing but to preserve it, and does so with the greater desire, as the joy is greater',[27] it follows that those employees who are most deeply caught up in the net of this particular form of passionate servitude occupy themselves joyfully in the service of a desire that appears not to be theirs, but which precisely the affective mechanism of the demand for love makes theirs. It serves no purpose to remain at the level of first impressions and to 'deride and bewail',[28] from the outside, these efforts that appear 'alienated' – 'how can anyone spend twelve hours a day engaged in management control and moreover enjoy it!?' These efforts are not alienated because they are, as it were, *foreign* to the subject as a solid core of autonomy (that subject does not exist), a subject remaining 'separated from itself', in the mysterious form of being 'a stranger to oneself' that pre-Althusserian readings of Marx sometimes revisit. The subordinate's desire to meet the desire of the superior in order to please the superior and to be loved in return belongs incontestably to the subordinate and there is nothing 'foreign' in it. That it was not originally the subordinate's desire matters little. No desire is 'original', and this desire will become well and truly the subordinate's own. The only alienation is that of passionate servitude. But this is universal, and cannot be used to make objective distinctions between people.

VOCATIONAL IMAGES

Consent in employment is not limited to the form of the local-ised love affect, invested in a specific person. One can also be

---

27   *Ethics*, III, 37, Demonstration.
28   *Political Treatise*, I, 1.

led to desire outside the orbit of a particular inducer. There is ample evidence for that in the sociology of consumption, of tastes or of vocations, one could almost say in the whole discipline, to the extent that it concerns itself with socialisation as the incorporation of norms – namely, of manners of behaving, hence of desiring to behave. It is impossible to untangle the immense work of self-affection that society incessantly performs on itself, producing norms, things to want, vocations to embrace, glories to pursue, etc. Desire without object, the conatus finds its objects in the social world, and chiefly in the spectacle of other conative surges, since, except for the passage of desire from one object to another by association or relatedness (*Ethics*, III, 15, Corollary), affective mimetism (*Ethics*, III, 27) is the most elementary mechanism that produces attachments to objects.

The word 'elementary' must be insisted upon so as to refute from the outset the idea that desire emerges from imitative interactions that are purely *bilateral*.[29] The phenomenology of interpersonal influences is merely the above-water part of a structure of relations of which individuals are local actualisations. To imitate a certain man is already to imitate a man, therefore not a woman. Thus the man in question becomes more or less imitable or inimitable (in the sense of not being the kind that should be imitated) for no other reason than his quality of being a man, therefore bearing the full weight of social relations of gender, and this without prejudice to all the other social qualities that the imitator perceives: is he white or black, rich or poor, young or old? Does he belong to one social group or sub-group rather than to another? Does he enjoy a particular reputation as a trendsetter; does he possess some symbolic capital that makes him an authoritative reference, etc.? In each

---

29   For a properly socio-institutional analysis of affective imitation in Spinoza, see Lordon, 'La puissance des institutions'.

case, what is expressed in those (social) qualities are social relations that determine effects of imitation, which from then on
have nothing strictly *interpersonal* about them beyond the
superficial level of their phenomenological appearing. This is
enough to give a sense of the complexity and drawn-out proliferation of the social and institutional mediations that concretely
effectuate the mimetic mechanism, for example those involved
in the production of symbolic capital, which establish certain
agents as exceptionally imitable. Such complexity poses a challenge to a synoptic presentation, leaving little choice other than
to simply say that the whole of society is involved in the tiniest
imitation of desire.

No doubt it can be pointed out that the impersonal in this
determination necessarily takes personalised roads, whether
in the form of real persons who are directly imitated, or of
fictional characters whose imitability passes through the power
of the story, a power described by Yves Citton as 'mythocratic,'
which is the power of the imagination – and we know the vocations, that is to say, the desired lives, which the latter is capable
of producing.[30] But what must be emphasised above all is that
this form of the production of desire has the specific character
of being determined by diffuse, delocalised, impersonal and
unattributable mechanisms, and is therefore more likely to be
overlooked or remain unconscious. One should rather say,
'*even* more likely', since Spinoza warns from the outset that our
awareness of our acts and desires does not extend to the causes
determining them, still less when these determinations are so
multiple, so drawn-out, and, one could say, so much the product of the individual's immersion in the whole social pool.
Already little inclined to think of themselves as determined,
desiring individuals are even more disposed to consider

30   Yves Citton, *Mythocratie. Storytelling et imaginaire de gauche*, Éditions
Amsterdam, 2010.

themselves the origins of their desires when both the complexity and the evanescence of the causal process that would have to be grasped make it particularly easy for them to remain unconscious of their desire's determination. Here there is neither localised amorous dependence nor personalised affective mimetism, but the unremitting process of innumerable exposures to social influences, at times infinitesimal, at times brutally decisive (experienced as a 'revelation'), for the full length of a trajectory of existence. By a truncation that optimises the cognitive economy, the fact of the felt desire imposes itself, alone, on consciousness, allowing the imagination to yield to the illusion of self-determination and the originary will. Those who love an activity – sales ('for the contact with clients'), auditing or financial analysis ('for the precision'), services ('for the relational quality') – or a sector – oil prospecting (high-risk venture), aviation (high tech), civil engineering (working outside) – or who seek the prestige of business accomplishments – success as measured by the job status, the monetary reward, or the executive lifestyle (burning the midnight oil, travel, sharp suits, deluxe accessories) – always speak of 'my choice', what 'I enjoy', 'my' lifelong vocation, and it matters little that the accumulation of affect-imbued images that constituted these things as objects of desire, and determined the enlistment through these choices of employment, came entirely from outside. The fact remains that these desires, induced from outside but turned into authentic internal desires, determine joyful commitments when they are given an opportunity for satisfaction by the line of employment that corresponds to them. In an expression that is now common despite meaning nothing at all, individuals 'fulfil themselves', which really means that they fulfil their desires. The reflexive form betrays the subjectivist illusion that, in completely assimilating the subject to its desire – since 'to fulfil oneself' and to 'fulfil one's desire' are the same thing – wants to foster the impression that this perfect coincidence depends on the subject being the exclusive origin of its desire. Having incurred this desire – evidently tailored for the organisation but now made their own – the individuals 'consent', and set themselves in motion joyfully, of their own accord.

Thus, among other things by its system of education, training, and career counselling, the whole society works to produce vocational images that pre-co-linearise individuals, making them future enlistees conditioned to desire enlistment. However, at the level of the whole this process is only partially intentional, since, except for the apparatus of career counselling which is explicitly dedicated to this task, the imaginary production of the larger society is not governable but takes place boundlessly, as a process without a subject, and with no prior deliberate correspondence to the requisites of the social division of capitalist labour – at times even against it, since one also finds in the stream of these vocational images the images of the poet, the traveller, the off-grid farmer, the artist who cannot be bought, and all the runaway figures, the good-for-nothing and the scofflaw.[31]

POSSESSION OF SOULS AS TOTALITARIANISM

The lesson of this is that pre-co-linearisation is far from perfect; more could be done to reduce the drift α. What the world outside the enterprise has failed to do, the enterprise will take upon itself to complete. It could have been satisfied with the work of the fundamental structures of the employment relation, those of monetary dependence, along with the general work of socialisation that pre-normalises young individuals to life as employees. But, as we saw, the mere *reduction* of the

---

31   And this even though capitalism puts all its inventiveness into trying, not always successfully, to reintegrate such runaways.

angle α is no longer sufficient for the enterprise. The neoliberal enterprise now seeks full alignment and the *annulation* of the drift, to obtain $\alpha = \emptyset$. Capital, freed from all restraints, is able to impose a new norm of enlistment, using the new requisites of economic activity – the pressure of external constraints imposed by shareholders and competition – as a pretext. In fact it is able to impose this norm only because the same structures that impose these 'constraints' are also those that alter the balance of power between capital and labour, making full alignment possible.

Coerced participation, which can be more aptly called over-mobilisation by sad affects, is not the end of the paradox of the neoliberal enterprise, which undertakes *at the very same time*, perhaps not to make itself loved, but to have its employees embrace its desire and thus to usher them into a regime of joyful affects.

The word 'embrace' must be understood in the most exacting sense, as perfection in adoption and adaptation. This is indeed represented by the limitlessness of the zero-α project. Apart from indicating a certain strategic situation, the delirium of the unlimited is therefore above all the seed of a new political form which we may very well call totalitarian, evidently not in the classic meaning of the term, but in that it aims at the *total* subordination of employees, more precisely, at their total *investment*. Subordinates are expected not only, according to the common formula, to 'fully invest themselves', but also to be fully invested – invaded – by the enterprise. Even more than the excesses of quantitative appropriation, it is the extreme nature of the hold claimed over individuals that is the hallmark of the neoliberal enterprise's pursuit of total enlistment. To subordinate the *entire* life and being of employees to the business, namely, to remake the dispositions, desires, and attitudes of enlistees so that they serve *its* ends, in short, to refashion their singularity so that all their personal inclinations tend 'spontaneously' in *its* direction, such is the delirious vision of a total *possession* of individuals, in an almost shamanistic sense. It is therefore legitimate to call totalitarian an attempt to exercise control in a manner so profound, so complete, that it is no longer satisfied by external enslavement – obtaining the desirable behaviour – but demands the complete surrender of 'interiority'. The neoliberal enterprise seeks perfect co-linearity, namely, adherence in the strongest sense of the word, making the vector *d* 'stick' to *D* without deviation. It wants to abolish the distinction between the individual and itself that is measured by desire and its tendencies – it wants, in other words, full *coincidence*.

Since it seeks the total identification of enlistees with its own ends as the condition of the complete capture of their power of acting, the neoliberal enterprise 'takes' individuals and appraises the degree of their pre-existing co-linearity. Some already walk on their own, spontaneously, in the desired direction; from the outset, they have attached their vital interests to the enterprise, interests that are existential in the broad sense, including not only monetary gain but also the achievement of a desired way of life. They are the top-level directors and upper management, for whom the professional life is almost synonymous with life as such. From the outset they exhibit therefore the best possible alignment with the ends of the organisation, which serves them as much as they serve it. The rest, who do not present the same degree of union, must be duly co-linearised a second time. To truly drive home the applicability of the term totalitarianism to an undertaking as mad as this tailored reconstruction of interiorities, desires, and attitudes, it is necessary to follow the example of Dardot and Laval and enter the inner sanctum of the 'manufacture of neoliberal subjects', going into the details of those 'human resources' programmes, what happens inside them and what individuals are made to do, and how far they go in attempting behavioural and affective re-education.[32] But only images can truly shock us, for example the documentary of Jean-Robert Viallet, which takes us inside the normalising hell of a call centre in which the quantitative control of timing is joined by the qualitative control of vocal intonations, or again inside a group 'workshop' in which, with seeming gentleness but in fact with even worse violence, managers are made to laugh or play games on command, and are enjoined to completely surrender their affectivity.[33] One of the most pathetic scenes, which is at the same time the only antidote against total despair, shows the 'human resources' manager, the facilitator of the 'workshop' of behavioural re-education, finally packing up his belongings, leaving the firm, and moving to another region with the hope of beginning 'a new life', as if the confused feeling of having taken part is something unbearable had become unbearable to him as well.

THE GIRLFRIEND EXPERIENCE
(AFTER THE GIFT OF TEARS)

The distinction between the successful endeavour of reconfiguring the desire of employees and the pure and simple enslavement of reconditioning is at times extremely tenuous. Winifred Poster reports on the astounding example of Indian workers in the outsourced call centre of a US service company, whose employer does not hesitate to compel them to take on a borrowed American identity in order to better 'relate' to clients.[34] Not only must the call centre employees speak English

---

32   Dardot and Laval, *La nouvelle raison du monde*, p. 77.

33   Jean-Robert Viallet, *La mise à mort du travail*, Part 2, 'L'aliénation', Yami2 Productions.

34   I borrow this example from David Alis, '"Travail émotionnel, dissonance émotionnelle et contrefaçon de l'intimité". Vingt-cinq ans après la publication de *Managed Heart* d'Arlie R. Hochschild', in Isabelle Berrebi-Hoffmann,

with an American accent and diction, but they also have to develop an interest in regional news (notably sports and the weather) from the part of the US they cover, so as to chat with their customers (they were also advised to watch *Friends*), and finally they must change their names (an Anil becomes an Arnold).[35] Examples of this kind give a fairly clear idea of the neoliberal utopia of the full makeover of individuals. Their extreme character should not obscure the general tendencies of the economic shift towards the service sector, where the productive performance is primarily a 'human' performance, namely, affective and behavioural. Pushing to the utmost the reification already inscribed in the vocabulary of economists ('labour factor') and shareholders ('human resources'), the master-desire of capital no longer makes a secret of the fact that it sees employees as endlessly malleable material, capable of being reshaped to any model that suits its requisites, thus revealing in this image the ultimate truth of the employment relation as a relation of instrumentalisation, a *reductio ad utensilium*. One must in fact go very far in denying individuals any inner consistency – at this stage no one dares even to mention grand terms such as 'dignity' – in order to find projects of identity remanufacturing of comparable scope.

But there is actually worse than the outsourced Indian call centre, in which, after all, employees still have some room to resist the colonisation of their personhood by keeping the behavioural script at a distance, as a role to enact, which allows them to recover the integrity of their persons once the 'performance' is over. There is worse indeed every time an enterprise in the service sector not only commands employees to show the

---

Politiques de l'intime. Des utopies sociales d'hier aux mondes du travail d'aujourd'hui, La Découverte, 2009. Poster's original article is 'Who's on the Line? Indian Call Center Agents Pose as Americans for US-Outsourced Firms', *Industrial Relations* 46, n° 2 (2007).

35   Alis, 'Travail émotionnel', p. 231.

required emotions (empathy, attention, solicitude, smiling), but aims at the ultimate behavioural performance in which the prescribed emotions are no longer merely outwardly enacted, but 'authentically' felt. This in fact closely resembles the practices of the seventeenth-century Church, which, in giving its absolution, no longer settled for contrition, the ritualised, outward expression of words, always suspected of hiding insincerity, but demanded attrition, the presence in the confessed of an authentic love of God from which the words must flow, namely, an 'internal' disposition.[36] With this, in keeping with its historical dynamics and with the goal of universal propagation of the faith that gave it its name, *katholikos*, the Church was merely extending to the mass of believers practices previously reserved for the virtuosos or the elect, such as the gift of tears,[37] understood as the external sign of an affective interiority authentically inhabited by grace.

Through a leap in time that is in fact a continuous expansion, neoliberal capitalism inherits this long historical labour and adds its own extensions by putting, so to speak, the gift of tears on the agenda of the whole class of employees. But this deliberate attempt to generalise virtuosity encounters a number of difficulties. Since the sincerity of first-person experience is perceived as the guarantee of authenticity, hence of the emotional quality of the provided service, companies do not hesitate to throw their employees into the inevitable *double bind* that consists in attempting to manufacture artlessness. On command, the 'smile must be "true", coming from "the bottom of the heart."'[38] And the human material – a term that should definitely be preferred to that of 'human resources', which still falls short of the truth – must contend as it can with these

---

36   Jean Delumeau, *L'aveu et le pardon*, Fayard, 1990.
37   Piroska Nagy, *Le don des larmes au Moyen-Âge*, Albin Michel, 2000.
38   Alis, 'Travail émotionnel', p. 227.

contradictions of spontaneity on command and naturalness on demand. But the Christian idea of the gift of tears no longer resonates with contemporaries, who are looking for other references – and will find them. It is a safe bet that if one day, following a change in customs and regulations, prostitution leaves the underworld to become an official trade, any company entering that market will expect its employees to kiss, and then to love, for real. Neoliberal capital is the world of the *girlfriend experience*.

THE INSCRUTABLE MYSTERY OF ENLISTED DESIRE

At times, remoulding individuals and transforming them into affective robots leaves a strange aftertaste. The other face of neoliberal utopia, the laughing and charmed one, would rather take the form of a beautiful, spontaneous community of *identically* desiring individuals. This fantasy is as crucial in the mind .of capital's recruiting sergeants as that of liquidity. But it is a fantasy that is yet to be achieved, for a corrosive doubt never ceases to weigh upon it. This enlistee swears that he has no other passion than the manufacture of yogurt, our company's business, but can we unreservedly believe him? Recruiters rediscover daily the difference that Marx identified in theory between labour and labour-power, and the always problematic conversion of the second into the first. Since the purchase of labour-power does not guarantee its effective future mobilisation, the enlister must deal with the irreducible doubt that continues to taint this actualisation. Of course, the enlistees will go through the co-linearisation machine. But everyone knows that the makeover of desires is uncertain work; it can even face recalcitrance, and its effectiveness is inversely proportional to the size of the deviation α that it must reduce. Therefore the measurement of the initial level of co-linearisation of enlistees acquires a strategic importance to which the practices of recruitment in a way testify. 'Can he join our community of desire?' This is the nagging question that haunts the recruitment procedure, at least as much as the evaluation of skills. For technical know-how is nowadays secondary, or almost. On the one hand it is assumed that, having acquired generic learning capacities in the course of their school years and university education, the newly recruited can be trained in the specific skills they will need by the company itself. On the other hand, what use are these technical skills unless activated by an animating desire? Yet the latter depends on an individual who remains an enigma.

In the lexicographical order of requisites, desire, as the force that mobilises the body and the mind, decidedly occupies the top hierarchical position, and all other entries are subordinate to it. However, before individuals can be thrown into the co-linearisation machine, their desiring temperament presents recruiters with its irreducible opacity and inscrutable mystery: 'What does this one really love? What would really move her?' Or more exactly, 'Will our own things really move her?' Of course, candidates are perfectly conscious of the investigation of which they are the object. So they invariably adopt the same strategy, declaring their interest in advance as a kind of legal minimum of desiring conformity, commonly referred to as 'intent' – 'That interests me a lot, I am fascinated by . . .' – whose stereotypical quality is most clearly revealed when reversed in parody. Performance artist Julien Prévieux provides a fine example with the letters of non-application that he sends in response to job offers: 'I write to you following your ad in the journal *Carriers and Jobs*. I swear I never did anything wrong . . . I don't do drugs. I love animals. I don't steal. I buy mass-produced goods like everybody else. I exercise to keep healthy. Later I would like to have a kid or two and a dog. It is also my intention to become a property owner and buy stocks. I have witnesses who saw me not doing anything.

I don't know what I'm guilty of. I don't know why you want to punish me with forced labour on databases . . . I kindly ask you not to hire me.' Alternatively, he sends a declaration of pre-normalisation, perfect to the point of caricature, but topped with an incomprehensible Bartleby-style desire: 'I would prefer not to.' The automated reply, from an anonymous bureaucracy that misses the point completely and squares the stereotype, is just as comical: 'We appreciate your trust in our company . . . Despite all the interest in your candidacy, we regret to inform you that we are unable to offer you a position. Although your education and experience generally meet the requirements of the job, other candidates present a better fit. Yours, etc.'[39] It is worth noting that, except for the punch line, Prévieux's letters of non-application are less the declaration of a specific interest than the affirmation of an overall social normalisation, put forward as a generic predisposition to the life of employment, incidentally an illustration of the congruence between employment for wages and an entire social order. We do not live merely in a capitalist economy, but in a capitalist *society*.

But more is needed to convince an employer: notably, one must supply proof of authentic desires specific to the firm. Certain sectors are more disposed to 'passion', and in them the investigation (by the employer) and the proof (by the employee) are relatively easy. This is the case, for example, with the sale of sporting goods, where employers know that they can count on sport enthusiasts, assumed to be 'authentically passionate.'[40] No doubt without seeing it as a sufficient condition, businesses can at least expect to make these employees more pliable to the discipline of employment,

---

39   Julien Prévieux, *Lettres de non-motivation*, Archon, 2000.

40   See William Gasparini, 'Dispositif managérial et dispositions sociales au consentement. L'exemple du travail de vente d'articles de sport', in Durand and Le Floch (eds), *La question du consentement au travail*.

since it is mitigated by an environment of loved objects that recall loved personal activities. Not all economic sectors however benefit from such a fortunate overlap with hobbies that generate individual passions. Outside these fairly special cases, declarations of interest are more suspect, or at least require more intensive scrutiny. How to probe candidates' dispositions, ascertain the orientations of their power of acting, and be fully confident of their adequate auto-mobility? We cannot hope to exhaust the inventory of extravagant practices, sometimes verging on delirium, deployed by human resources managers in an effort to pierce that hard core of desiring individuality, an irredeemably irrational endeavour that is therefore doomed to every folly. The transformation in recruiting methods that took place over the last two decades encapsulates all by itself the contemporary transformations of capitalism and notably that of its regime of mobilisation. The old selection methods, almost automatable, resting on simple criteria of training and experience, suitable for precisely defined jobs that can be broken down into well-specified basic tasks, retreated before forms of investigation that target dispositions, in accord with today's jobs, which are defined by their objectives ('projects') and leave to 'autonomous' employees the initiative of inventing the operative modes to achieve them. Increasingly generic job descriptions call for equivalent methods of employee selection, namely, by generic behavioural competences much more than by specific technical specifications. However, whereas the appreciation of technical competences is amenable to at least some rationalisation, that of behavioural competences is infinitely less so. Yet the pressure of discovering in advance what can only be known after the fact and through the very experience of working is so strong that everything must be tried, however nonsensical: role playing (supposedly revelatory), inquisitional interrogations about normally irrelevant matters (but the personal life must harbour precious information, since it is 'the full person' that needs to be assessed), experimental protocols that are almost behaviourist (to test the subject's reactions), graphology (the secrets of personality lurk in downstrokes and upstrokes), even physiognomy (plump means lazy), numerology (numbers don't lie), and astrology (neither do planets). Although they have somewhat improved after the first phase of delirious excess in the 1980s and '90s, recruitment practices remain at the edge of unreason, to which they are inevitably doomed by their impossible aims. And since the verification of the degree of pre-co-linearisation will always come up against this insurmountable limit, it is the enterprise that is left with the task of perfecting the alignment as much as it can, to produce individuals who conform their desires to its own.

THERE IS NO INTERIORITY
(AND NO INTERIORISATION EITHER)

To make others' desire like the master-desire is the utterly simple secret of light-hearted, even joyful, obedience. We could speak of 'interiorisation' if we so wish; but despite its familiarity, the term creates more problems than it solves. For consent always points back to the authenticity of the subject, the subject's *core*, which – the very language suggests it quite explicitly – is to be found 'inside'. But what distinguishes between consent and coercion is not topology – exterior versus interior – but the nature of the affects, sad or joyful, that are respectively associated with each.

It is the fault of the Cartesian dead ends to have spread such confusion by making interiority one of the defining elements of the metaphysics of subjectivity. Yet it is Descartes who first posits the substantial difference between Extension and Thought. Besides, up to that point Spinoza is in his own way a

Cartesian – but only up to that point.[41] Extension and Thought are two orders of expression of Being – unlike Descartes, Spinoza will not call them *substances* but *attributes*[42] – that are absolutely heterogeneous, and as such absolutely separate from each other. But Descartes fails to maintain the substantial difference between them. Turning back to the human person and wanting it to be a subject endowed with free will, Descartes searches for an improbable link between body and mind, which ruins the initial assumption of separation. For the soul to exercise sovereign command over the body, the two must interact somewhere and have a point of homogeneity. The pineal gland thus becomes this inextricable aporia of the corporeal site of the incorporeal soul. Spinoza does not abandon the unity of body and soul. On the contrary, he takes it to the highest level, since body and soul are for him *one and the same thing*, considered under the different attributes of Extension and Thought. But he abandons without regret (although at the cost of the most severe incomprehension) any causal interaction between them, and therefore also any need for finding a site common to both. Produced by the encounters between bodies, affects inscribe themselves first in bodies, as variations in their power of acting; this corporality, that puts the 'psychology of emotions' back in the mortal coil, is not the least characteristic sign of the Spinozist difference. However, while Spinoza certainly

---

41   Pascal Gillot correctly stresses the difference between Descartes' thought and the wider movement of thought that one can call Cartesianism. For, beyond its eponymous author, Cartesianism can be conceived as the raising of a problem, that of the relations between body and soul, that 'Cartesians', not all of whom affiliate themselves with Descartes, made theirs, but each giving this problem its own solution. In this respect, despite all that separates them from Descartes, Malebranche, Spinoza and Leibniz are Cartesians in their way. See Pascale Gillot, *L'esprit, figures classiques et contemporaines*, CNRS Éditions, 2007.

42   And the difference is not just words, since considerable differences follow from imagining multiple substances as does Descartes, or multiple attributes of the same substance as does Spinoza.

understands affects as 'affections of the body by which the body's power of acting is increased or diminished',[43] he also sees them as 'at the same time, the ideas of these affections.'[44] Thus, *in so far as* they are ideas of the body's affections, affects *also* have a mental part. But because these ideas belong to the attribute Thought, and in so far as this attribute is absolutely distinct from the attribute *Extension*, they – our feelings or states of mind, as much in the common usage as in the Spinozist sense – are strictly *without a site*: localisation only applies to things that have extension, from which ideas in general, as well as the particular ideas of our affections, are excluded by definition. Consequently our states of mind, barring patent absurdity, cannot be said to be in any way 'interior', since 'interior' is a topological indication and topology is limited to the attribute Extension. From the fact that states of mind cannot be seen by an outside observer, yet are nevertheless experienced by the subject, it has been deduced that they cannot be anywhere but inside the subject, concealed in its mortal coil and veiled by its opacity: thus the Cartesian neurosciences, confusing mind with brain (often unknowingly and without the slightest hesitation), 'logically' continue to search for them 'inside'.[45]

Since the idea of consent makes common cause with that of interiority, both prove to be meaningless together. Coercion, which is the opposite of consent, collapses in front of the same aporia, and likewise the polar opposites of imposition and legitimacy, *hard power* and *soft power*, and so on. The point is not that these antinomies correspond to *nothing* – those who experience the situations in which these words come up know very well how to distinguish between them! Rather, the terms distort precisely what they seek to capture. None of these opposites

---

43   *Ethics*, III, Definition 3.

44   Ibid.

45   But not all neuroscience is like this: see Antonio Damasio, *L'Erreur de Descartes*, Odile Jacob, 1995.

correspond to the deceptive difference between exterior force and (evidently sovereign) interior assent, as their common usage (and often learned discourse as well) implies. For one is determined to assent just as one is determined to suffer: whichever state of mind one is in, it is always the product of exo-determination, and *from this standpoint* all states of mind are strictly alike. But only from this standpoint; in other respects they are very different, and it is not for nothing that they make those who experience them say sharply contrasting things, such as 'I consent' versus 'I yield'. Their true difference however always comes back to the fundamental polar opposition between the joyful and the sad. One can see a sign of the displacement of this difference in the double meaning of words such as 'enthralled' and 'captivated', which refer both to tyrannical enslavement and to enchanted acquiescence. In both cases one is indeed chained – to the order of causal determination – but with opposite affects in each. The difference is surely not minor, but nor is it what it is commonly believed to be – in any case it is not the difference between the free will that says yes wholeheartedly and the one that was temporarily made to yield by a superior force. Those who consent are no freer than anyone else, and are no less 'yielding' than the enslaved; only, they have been made to yield differently and thus experience their determination joyfully. There is no consent, in the same way that there is no voluntary servitude. There are only happy subjections.

Joyful affects, however, are not especially conducive to thinking. 'There is always the violence of a sign that forces us into the search, that robs us of peace,' writes Deleuze, reminding us that thinking is more likely to be set in motion by an unpleasant encounter, namely, by a sad affect.[46] As if by a sort of self-sufficiency of joy, felicity raises few questions. That is why

---

46   Gilles Deleuze, *Proust and Signs*, University of Minnesota Press, 2004.

the forgetting of exo-determination, already inscribed in the intuitive truncations of the knowledge of the first type, is even deeper when the causes that are ignored are those of joyful affects. Top executives do not go to work less alienated than their subordinates. They have passively undergone the social pre-normalisation that disposed them to the life of employment. They are not the origin of the vocational images that guided their educational trajectories and their professional choices (and even less of the social conditions that made these trajectories and choices possible). They have thus been determined as much as anyone else to experience the desire that animates them. The difference is simply that they are animated joyfully, that is to say, under the effect of a desire to obtain a good rather than to avoid an evil, and by its affects of hope that are strong enough for them to surrender completely to this desire and to experience it as their own sovereign wish. In these joyful situations, even less than in other circumstances, the idea of the heteronomy of desire has not the slightest chance to cut a path for itself inside the mind of the desiring individual. Desire is never *of* me and yet always *mine*, in other words, it never originates exclusively within desiring individuals but is nevertheless absolutely theirs – the 'I am the one desiring' is incontestable. In the case of joyful affects this ambivalence of desire is therefore even more doomed to the disavowal that throws the 'not of me' into oblivion, keeping only the 'mine'.

THE RISKS OF THE CONSTRUCTIVISM OF DESIRE

The ease with which heteronomy escapes consciousness is proportional to the complexity of the process of determination. Even the best introspective intention is unable to recollect all the innumerable biographical affections (encounters, influences, exposures) that have sedimented within a desiring temperament. The awareness of having experienced a desire obliterates every other consideration, especially that of know-ing what determined it. Why does this person have the desire to occupy herself as a financier, while that other contracted the desire to be a dancer? Neither of them will have more than a very partial understanding of it, and of little value anyway in their eyes.

There are no doubt desires whose *proximate* cause can be identified – even if what determined the disposition to be responsive to that *particular* cause remains unknown. The typi-cal situation is that of localised imitation (whose generative scheme is given in *Ethics*, III, 27): I make mine the desire of another whom I recognise as imitable. One could almost use an epidemiological metaphor: I catch this desire from contact with someone else, who gives it to me. What led me to recognise that imitability – the social properties of the person imitated, the circumstances of the encounter between us, the love I have for that person (whatever its form) – will probably remain in the dark. But the immediate origin of this desire can be conscious: I am aware of the fact that I desire in conformity with that other person, that I want this because of, and sometimes for, that person. This kind of desire is surrounded with affects of love; how could it not be joyful? And how could the desiring subject not feel intensely that this desire, although tied to another, absolutely belongs to the subject, an expression of its most sovereign will? It is the suggestions or commands to desire coming from a hated other that give the subject the sense of an encroachment on what it imagines as its free will, thus allowing a dim awareness of exo-determination. But only the sad affect that comes from loathing the inducer accounts for the subject's rebellion against the external bending of its will, and the reac-tive movement to restore what it sees as its desiring sovereignty merely substitutes one determination for another, but with new affects that are joyful rather than sad. This is akin to the adoles-cent described by Spinoza, who, slamming the door of the family home to flee the authority of his parents, chooses to enlist in the army, thus preferring – but 'in total freedom', naturally – 'the discipline of an absolute commander in preference to . . . the admonitions of a father'.[47]

Can the institutional inducement of desire produce similar effects? More precisely, under what conditions can institutions succeed in inducing desires, and under what circumstances do their efforts provoke rejection? But first, who would deny the existence of constructivist[48] projects of desire (namely, the existence of institutional epithumogeneses)? Spinoza already observed that the state, rather than relying on fear, should seek to lead people so 'that they may think that they are not led, but living after their own mind, and according to their free decision.'[49] We can easily recognise in this maxim of political prudence the very aim of the neoliberal enterprise, another way of reminding us that the enterprise, being a gathering of powers of acting, falls fundamentally within the scope of political philosophy. 'Remaking' the desires of members of a body in order to conform them to the requisites of that body's perseverance is therefore not an entirely new idea. In the *Gorgias*, Plato even makes it one of the loftiest subjects of the art of politics and the yardstick by which Pericles' fault should be measured.[50] But, at least in the modern era, this endeavour has against it all the inconveniences of constructivism as the manifest, external intervention of a conditioning agency. The modern consciousness errs in reserving the imputation of conditioning to this kind of intention alone, since conditioning is merely another name for universal passionate servitude. But it sees right in that,

---

47   *Ethics*, IV, Appendix 13.
48   The term constructivism here is Hayek's. See Friedrich A. Hayek, 'The Persistence of Constructivism in Current Thought', in *Law, Legislation and Liberty*, Routledge, 2012. [Trans.]
49   *Political Treatise*, X, 8.
50   Plato, *Gorgias*, trans. Donald Zeyl, Hackett, 1986, 517 b-c.

even if we are conditioned in everything, the manner of acquiring these conditionings, or more precisely the question of knowing whether there are identifiable bodies that condition and even intentions to condition, makes a difference.

Thus, for example, it is fair to say that at a very general level society as a whole works by self-affection to shape the desires and the affects of its members.[51] But this process of self-affection of society remains unassignable, except nominally to the broadest agency which is society itself; it carries no intention, no deliberate design. Utterly without a *telos*, it is so vast and, crucially, so diffuse, so devoid of a centre, that it appears to individuals – when it appears to them at all – as a necessity over which none has any real control. It follows that, strictly speaking, this kind of conditioning can no longer be called constructivism. The impersonalisation and delocalisation of the process of collective self-affection provides it with the best means to make itself imperceptible, or indeed tolerable, even as it nevertheless produces normalisation effects that are no less intense, and at times even painful. 'Given an equal cause of love, love toward a thing will be greater if we imagine the thing to be free than if we imagine it to be necessary. And similarly for hate.'[52] Spinoza touches here on the affective mechanism that traces from the outset the limits of constructivist political projects, by implication also calling attention to the historical strength of capitalism, at least up to a certain point. What makes the constructivist agency a focal point for very intense affects of hate is the possibility of ascribing the conditioning to a local, identifiable cause, one that is thought to be free (the Party, the State, the Central Planning Committee), and to which a contingent intentionality can be imputed. In contrast, capitalism's

---

51   On the idea of the self-affection of the multitude, see Lordon, 'L'empire des institutions'.

52   *Ethics*, III, 49.

market forces, despite grinding people down no less violently, appear as a 'systemic effect', thus unassignable, without a centre and without deliberate design behind them; they seem almost like a necessity, which for Marx was the essence of commodity fetishism, and thereby conducive to all the rhetorical strategies that depoliticise things by naturalising them.[53]

Seen in this way, the neoliberal enterprise certainly takes risks: the risks of relocalisation, of its intentionality becoming assignable and its constructivism made visible again and all the more exposed to the hate that is reserved to free causes, since its capturing intention is so patent. Yet there have been earlier institutions that strove to construct the 'interiority' of their subjects, and did so in the most visible of manners. The Catholic Church is evidently the first example that comes to mind. It is true that its particular institutional history is intimately tied to the history of the formation of subjectivity, and that the (imaginary) idea of interiority is to a large degree its very invention, and emerged precisely when it undertook to take control of it. In a somewhat cursory and intuitive fashion, it can be suggested that the condition of possibility for this intense work on interiorities, which took place during (and drove) the first stages in the history of individualism, was undoubtedly the still very strong hold of tradition and authorities over individuals, and the latter's still embryonic belief in their autonomy as subjects. This disposed them to tolerate being the objects of such a fashioning, which was only in keeping with that intermediate

---

53   Episodes of intense crisis, such as the one that began in 2007, and the search for those 'in charge' and their inevitable 'responsibility' are needed in order to expose – provided that the search is carried out well – the hidden identities of those running the system and the role of particular interest groups in the contingent construction of 'necessity'. For the participation of the financial industry in setting up its own rules of the game, see Simon Johnson, 'The Quiet Coup', *The Atlantic*, theatlantic.com, 2009; Frédéric Lordon, *La crise de trop*, Fayard, 2009, Chapter 1.

historical phase of larval and inchoate individualism. It is a whole other 'material', more difficult to work with, that the neoliberal enterprise has under its hands, and its goal of remaking the desires and dispositions of its subjects thus collides headlong with their understanding of themselves precisely as subjects, namely, as beings endowed with an autonomy of desire such that any outside intervention runs the risk of being seen as an interference.

AMOR FATI CAPITALISTIS

People imagine themselves as subjects although they are nothing of the sort, and too visible a manipulation of their desiring temperament inevitably generates tensions. Hence the affective constructivism of the neoliberal enterprise encounters serious obstacles from the outset, and struggles to fully conceal the violence in the 'consent' it produces. In matters of desire and affects, constructivist violence is first of all the violence of its very *telos*, the violence of the alignment with the master-desire. For one can hardly find a more purposive normalisation than that of the neoliberal enterprise. Its production of desires and affects is not left to the unassignable causalities of a process without a subject; there is a head, and it knows what it wants. Of all capitalist epithumogeneses, the practice called coaching – that acme of subjectivising normalisation one would think our era had specially tailored to fit Michel Foucault's intellectual legacy – goes the furthest in undertaking the makeover of affective temperaments. It therefore also registers in the most violent way the tensions of the contradiction between the formal objectives of 'personal development' and 'empowerment', and the real objectives of narrow conformity to behavioural specifications that reproduce the sponsoring enterprise's specific imperatives of productivity and profitability. The most lucid coaches – or the least reticent – are quite conscious of that tension and admit it without too many circumlocutions: the primary goal of their intervention with the 'coachee' is to 'transform an exogenous pressure into an endogenous motivation', as one of them states, with either perfect honesty or perfect candour.[54] Management-speak aside, it is impossible not to recognize in this project of transforming an exogenous requisite into an 'endogenous motivation' Spinoza's maxim, addressed to the sovereign: lead subjects so 'that they think that they are not led . . . but living after their own mind, and according to their free decision'. To induce an aligned desire is the perennial goal of bossing, namely, of all the institutions of capture. For the enlistees in the grip of the co-linearisation machine, the task is therefore to convert external imperatives, those of the enterprise and its particular objectives, into joyful affects and a personal desire, a desire that ideally they can each call their own. To produce consent is to produce in individuals a love for the situation in which they have been put. Neoliberal epithumogenesis is therefore the undertaking to produce *amor fati*; but not just any *fatum* – only its own, which it brings down on employees in the depths of heteronomy.

Even the 'coaches' must sense the gulf between the mandate entrusted to them by the sponsor, to generate love for a fate of serving productivity, and the humanist rhetoric of self-improvement with its hotchpotch of liberatory psychoanalysis and the Stoic's care of the self. Whatever the methods, the epithumogenic practices of the enterprises cannot hide their profoundly *adaptive* purpose and their true aim of leading enlistees to individual accommodation and even, beyond that, to the transfiguration of coercion, but outside any attempt to question it. Even the least controlling of these practices is open to the same objection. Take the coaching of top managers, who are already the most involved in their work, and with whom the

---

54   Laurence Baranski, *Le manager éclairé, pilote du changement*, Éditions d'Organisation, 2001, citing Guilhaume, *L'ère du coaching*.

coaches can permit themselves the luxury of merely proposing templates that appear very open and respectful of their subjects' 'autonomy': 'I've never been in a situation where I presented a problem and got an answer,' explains a high-level trainee; 'I described a problem, and got questions bounced back to me, which enabled me . . . to find the elements of a solution myself.'[55] But this is because these subjects of coaching are already considerably co-linearised, thus led to spontaneously carry out their introspective work under the guiding scheme of a master-desire that remains hidden in the thoughtlessness of the self-evident, and is therefore exempt from any questioning, before or after – the wonderful ease of pre-adjustment of the great auto-mobiles. For it would be quite something if at the end of the introspective analysis of their 'lack of empathy for subordinates', difficulty in 'managing relations with superiors', 'difficulties communicating' or 'stepping up to meet challenges', the long process of 'self-improvement' brought some coachees to the critical realisation that the situations in which they had been put were at times simply impossible, so that – the ultimate failure of coaching – they would turn against the capitalist enterprise when the goal was only to turn them inward.

If one were therefore to point to a secondary characteristic of the capitalist epithumogenesis (but how secondary is it really?), it would be the attempt to suppress at all costs any movement of extrospection, namely, to prevent individuals from turning their gaze to the external forces that take hold of them and to keep them firmly within the exclusive register of introspection, as a way of instilling in them that what happens to them inside the enterprise cannot be called into question – only how they will deal with it can.

Bound by design to neglect the duty of intransitivity that requires the work of reflexivity to be carried out for its own

---

55 Cited in Guilhaume, *L'ère du coaching*, p. 107.

sake, the production of the *amor fati capitalistis* offers one of the most underhand examples of what everyday language calls conditioning. Thus common sense does not err when it is given the (rare) opportunity to see, for example, thanks to a documentary, what these 'motivational' practices (workshops, conventions, etc.) look like, which only the goal distinguishes from overtly sect-like practices, and sometimes by very little.[56] As if to confirm the hypothesis of universal passionate servitude, the most surprising thing is that companies (sometimes) open their doors to cameras, no doubt because the filmmakers were persuasive enough, but also under the effect of a kind of perfectly innocent good conscience, whose source is management's own straightforward assent to what they do – unaware of any blatant affective instrumentalisation or mental manipulation, thus seeing no reason to dissimulate. This primary adherence reveals how much the conditioners are themselves conditioned and steeped in the same imaginary and the same passionate universe as those on whom they impose their desire, thus providing another powerful illustration of Bourdieu's remark, that the dominators are dominated by their very domination.

THE VEIL OF JOYFUL AFFECTS, THE BACKDROP OF SAD AFFECTS

Contradictorily, after lecturing the enlistees about *their* desire and *their* joy (at being offered the opportunity to pursue it), the work of co-linearisation must make them forget not only its ingrained transitivity and subservience to the capitalist master-desire, but also the backdrop of sad affects that always muddles

---

56   See Gérald Caillat and Pierre Legendre, *Dominus Mundi. L'empire du management*, DVD, Idéale Audience, ARTE France; Viallet, *La mise à mort du travail*.

its promise of joyful ones, the backdrop of sanctions and threats that forever accompanies the employment relation. For all the subjects of co-linearisation whose alignment still falls significantly short, normalisation proceeds under an impending sanction, for the failure of normalisation is not an option. The persistent deviants – in the literal sense of conatus-vector geometry – will meet the fate that the enterprise reserves to those who refuse it the promise of 'giving it their all'. The only choice it will give them is to undergo a makeover, so that they can give it all *with joy*. Instantaneously tearing away the veil of joyful desire, the failure to induce desire, the imperfect adaptation, and the incomplete accommodation at once bring back the iron fist of the employment relation, whether in the form of downward social mobility, demotion-reassignment, or, finally, pure and simple dismissal. The co-linearised are thus enjoined by the enterprise, but even more so by themselves, to convert to the joyful affects of the suitable desire, or else face the overwhelming affects of fear associated with the basal dependence and the threat to their bare life. Out of this 'depth' of the epithumogenic scene, with the backdrop of the asymmetric power relation forever behind the front-stage of happy co-linearisation, emerge the tensions of the *double bind* that tear the co-linearised apart: 'desire it yourself but only as I say; be autonomous but under my guidance', all variants of the canonical form 'be spontaneous'. And the only recourse is to use one's capacity for autosuggestion and re-enchantment so as to avoid acknowledging being bludgeoned into submission – when autosuggestion does not reach a pathological level.

That is why efforts of co-linearisation are never sure of success, and their effects cannot but diverge widely according to the different subjects they operate on. Taking into consideration local statistical anomalies, this effectiveness gradient is by and large indexed on the hierarchical position of the co-linearised, namely, on the degree of their proximity to the master-desire. At the very top of the hierarchy, individuals are pre-aligned to such an extent that effectiveness is maximal and the epithumogenic work is mostly methodological: its purpose is not to incite a desire which they possess almost in full already, but to marginally rearrange their passionate life so as to allow them to pursue it more effectively than they already willingly do on their own. In extreme cases the alignment relation is almost reversed: the individuals use the organisation to satisfy their own passionate goals.

In one of the rare texts in which he addresses the question of desire – and in the minor form of the introductory dialogue – Bourdieu invokes the case where 'agents exploit institutions to satisfy their urges'.[57] At issue is the relation between the institution of the Church and individuals whose passionate temperament pushes them to find in the pastoral vocation certain psychic profits, such as charisma, power over souls, mediating the divine, etc., that are a constant cause of concern for the Church, as they may indicate the presence of a violent passion that could lead the (future) pastor astray. Like any other master-desire, the institution of the Church cares about the conformity of its enlistees. But in complete opposition to the business enterprise, which worries about lack of 'motivation', the Church looks askance at excesses of zeal: the word for clerical normality, 'idoneity', designates the optimal point between necessary and excessive commitment. For the Church has less to fear from vocational deficiency – rarely does one enter a seminary against one's will – than from the passionate over-investment of 'fatal subjectivism',[58] an excess of passion that inclines 'ardent souls,

---

57   'Avant-propos dialogué', in Jacques Maître, *L'autobiographie d'un paranoïaque*, Anthropos, 1994, p. vi.

58   Joseph Lahitton, *Deux conceptions divergentes de la vocation sacerdotale. Exposé. Controverse. Conséquences pratiques*, Lethielleux, 1910, cited by Maître, *L'autobiographie*, p. 16.

more prone to enthusiasm and illusion'[59] to embrace the vocation under the spell of its 'attraction'.[60] Such individuals respond too strongly to the particular form of interest proposed to them by an institution that, as an institution of symbolic power, is conscious of functioning through interest, and, given its profession of disinterested faith, is wary of being represented by individuals who are *too visibly* interested.

It follows that the passionate transactions that develop between individuals and institutions can be more symmetrical that the 'simple' unilateral normalisation of the former by the latter. This can also be seen in a way in the social production of vocational imaginaries, for example in the case of activities most people consider repellent, such as geriatric medicine or embalming, but that nevertheless manage to positively attract a few by resonating with very deep elements of their passionate temperament or their drives. The business enterprise knows it can count on 'ardent souls'; unlike the Church, it seeks them out. For these souls, who are invested in the enterprise as much as it is in them, basic co-linearisation is immediate, although secondary realignments are still needed. But that is not how it goes, far from it, for all those subjected to neoliberal co-linearisation, especially when their passionate temperament does not suit the enterprise a priori to the degree reached by these great auto-mobiles. Acting for and on behalf of the enterprise cannot be taken for granted when the subjects' desire is not aligned from the outset. In these cases the alignment process always carries the risk of being experienced, either as simple coercion, or in the confused manner of a proposition that is marred by its backdrop of threat despite being worthy of consideration in its own right. Only a sociology of the employment relation could however shed light on the formation of such

---

59   Ibid.
60   Ibid.

dispositions of recalcitrance or vexed acceptance, and on how these dispositions would respond to an assignable co-linearising intentionality, one that moreover has the power to sanction them.

Outside these polar cases of 'ardent souls' and 'unruly souls', ordinary passionate life is marked, as Spinoza notes, by 'mixed feelings', namely, by the conflict of antagonistic affects; 'the mind vacillates' – *fluctuatio animi* – according to constantly recalculated affective resultants. The 'consent' that was once given keeps getting diluted and can at any moment fall apart as a result of new affections (events in the course of employment) that generate new affects. For in the actual moment of consent there is never more than the confrontation, internal to the psyche, between joyful affects and sad affects, following the elementary law of power according to which 'an affect cannot be restrained or taken away except by an affect opposite to, and stronger than, the affect to be restrained.'[61] Yet co-linearisation, especially when it is as marked with intentionality as neoliberal alignment is, can never fully dodge its saddening part, not so much because of the initial heterogeneity of desires and the fact that one desire aims at pulling the other in its direction, as because this reduction of one desire to the other does not take the form of a 'free' proposition, but always relies on an impending threat. Of course employees can be induced or led to be passionate about management auditing, the sale of forklifts, or catalytic cracking; of course they can seize all the opportunities for joy that the enterprise takes care to present them with – promotion, socialising, or the promise of 'self-fulfilment.' Yet despite all that, every now and then they can harbour other thoughts.

---

61   *Ethics*, IV, 7.

CHAPTER THREE

Domination, Liberation

RETHINKING DOMINATION THROUGH CONSENT

Consent is thus most often tainted by a violence arising from the fact that it is strictly oriented towards the service of an external master-desire, and because it is obtained against a backdrop of a threat. There are nevertheless cases in which it manifests itself in the form of nearly pure complexes of joyful affects, almost unblemished by sad affects that are too weak to modify the overall feeling that one is moving according to a perfectly authentic personal desire. How then to continue speaking of domination when those concerned smile so innocently at their imposed employment? Calling attention to the rampant intentionality and the capture of effort by the master-desire is of no use, since the person would respond with a 'This is really my choice' that puts an end to the discussion. It is equally useless to suggest the idea of alienation, first because the person's very affects offer a formal rebuttal, disproving the idea of their being a victim of a violence coming from outside, and because, as if by a practical Spinozist intuition, the recipient of the diagnosis of alienation could easily turn it against the questioner. For what privilege forbids imputing the same alienation to the latter, whose own enlistment seems to be experienced just as joyfully? Is not alienation subject to the same distortions as ideology, the latter polemically reduced to 'what other people think', while the former made to designate 'other people's passionate life'? To this the Spinozist would add the crucial point that passionate servitude is a universal condition, and to say that only some suffer from it reveals at least as much about the speakers as it does about those they describe.

But what remains of domination once alienation is universal and accompanied by joyful effects? Certainly, domination can still be defined as the asymmetrical relation arising from the fact that one person's pursuit of his or her desire passes through another. The dependence of an interest on another person makes the interested person *ipso facto* dominated and that other person dominating. Employees, for example, have no other way of satisfying their interests except by going through a 'buyer of labour-power'. But the employee's basal interest can be submerged under higher desires to which one's job offers real satisfaction, to the point that the objective relation of dependence leaves no affective trace and can be imagined as meeting the ideal set by the economic theory of symmetrical and mutually beneficial exchanges, a successful union of a master-desire and an individual desire in which the latter feels that it is above all serving itself, and not a master. Yet despite all the benefits that the individual draws from it, enlistment is not without cost. For however successful it is, the process of epithumogenesis has the effect, and in fact the intention, of *fixing* the enlistees' desire to a certain number of objects to the exclusion of others. Within capitalist organisations, the very function of hierarchical subordination is to assign each individual to a defined task according to the division of labour, namely, to an activity object that each must convert into an object of desire: 'Here is this very specific thing that you must desire doing.' The division of labour determines 'objectively' the tasks to be accomplished, whereas the relation of command distributes individuals to these tasks bi-jectively, riveting each to one exclusive task; the function of epithumogenesis is then to lead them to like it.

But there are many other things in which employees, conceived this time not as enlistees but as associates, could be interested, many things that exceed the narrow limits of an activity necessarily inserted in the division of labour, and that would pull them out of the latter towards higher usages of their power of acting. For example, rather than simply being subjected to it, employees may want to question the division of labour itself, that is, question the distribution of tasks, their remuneration, their organisation, and even beyond that, the general strategy of the enterprise, its fundamental political decisions, for example those relating to how to adapt to external pressures such as competition and the resulting allocation of effort in labour time, remuneration and headcount – in short, everything that concerns the destiny of the productive community of which they are full members and from which they can draw extended opportunities for joy. But the triplet division-of-labour/subordination/conditioning attaches the employees to an exclusive object of desire. Subjection, even when it is happy, consists fundamentally in *locking employees in a restricted domain of enjoyment*. The whole purpose of epithumogenic work is to orient the conatus of enlistees, by reconfiguring their imaginary and inducing joyful affects, towards narrowly defined objects that trace for it a new, well-determined perimeter of the desirable. Evidently, the very attempt to induce joyful affects implies a widening of the scope of the desirable relative to the employment relation's original passionate situation, which only offered evils to be avoided, not goods to be pursued. For the enterprise, the purpose of offering employees such benefits as the symbolic and material gains of promotion, a sense of belonging, and the prospects of recognition and love, is to widen the domain of interests in enlistment – and to facilitate co-linearisation. But this widening is meticulously controlled. For if desire must be stimulated or produced, it must under no circumstances escape the functional limits of the valorisation of capital and the social relations of subordination under which the latter takes place. Thus, even putting aside the original relation of dependence that imposes on employees to pass through it in the pursuit of their interests, the master-desire's success in leading the enlistees by giving them the feeling that they follow their own inclinations still retains its character of domination, although evidently under a form completely unlike naked coercion, since the enlistees keep assenting to it. This kind of domination can perhaps be redefined as *the effect that confers on some the ability to reserve to themselves possibilities (of enjoyment) and to divert others away from them.*

Breaking with the subjectivist aporiae of consent, one can therefore say that Bourdieu's symbolic violence, a soft domination that the dominated themselves 'consent' to, is a domination through joyful affects.[1] One can also connect the ethical-political implications of this concept to Spinoza's insistence that the complexity of the human body renders it capable of a large variety of expressions of its power of acting, and consequently, that it is very much in each person's interest to escape the fixations of the conatus and put this variety into effect: 'Whatever so disposes the human body that it can be affected in a great many ways, or renders it capable of affecting external bodies in a great many ways, is useful to man.'[2] It is precisely the deployment of this variety that life under the master-desire precludes, as the condition of the dominated produces the contraction of the domain of desire and its opportunities for joy. The distinctive feature of domination is thus to rivet the dominated to minor objects of desire, in any case those deemed so by the dominators, who keep the other objects for themselves. With joy rather than fear – this is no doubt how the dominators govern most effectively; but they delimit the joys strictly, rigorously selecting the objects of desire that will be offered. Determining the distribution of the desirable is therefore perhaps domination's most characteristic effect, and also the most general, since the spectrum of the desirable extends from the desire to avoid an evil to

---

1   Incidentally, symbolic violence is far from being limited to joyful affects, and its effects of classification, interdiction and belittlement can also produce sad affects (for example, of embarrassment or social shame).

2   *Ethics*, IV, 38.

the desire to win the greatest goods (the goods socially considered the greatest), passing through the desires for minor objects, sources of the humble joys that are reserved to the humble. Both 'hard domination' and 'soft domination' are thus included in this continuum of the desirable, the one *as much as* the other thinkable in the unified terms of desire and affects. They are distinguished only by the different affects, sad or joyful, by which they set bodies in motion.

THE DIVISION OF DESIRE AND
THE IMAGINARY OF POWERLESSNESS

The main stake of domination is distributive. To mix Weber's language with Spinoza's, one could say that its object is the distribution of the chances for joy. To put it this way is to point out both how far the spectrum of the joys of employment extends beyond the purely monetary – job titles, recognition, friendly socialising at work – and simultaneously how relatively narrow it is, limited to only those things that employees could in principle strive after in the context of their professional lives, not to mention outside it. The dominant distributive regulation that produces these adjusted desires and convinces the dominated that beyond these limits their ambitions are hopeless therefore requires, lest it degenerate into frustration, a continuous work of enchantment whose purpose is to persuade employees that their humble joys are 'really' great joys, in any case perfectly sufficient joys – for them. This work is all the more necessary since it must contend with the excesses of envy that the spectacle of the social world incessantly stokes and the *imatatio affectuum* that this spectacle never fails to induce: visibly, the great enjoy having certain things, which must therefore be very desirable, thus subject to the imitation of desire. Symbolic violence consists then properly speaking in the production of a double imaginary, the imaginary of fulfilment, which makes the humble joys to which the dominated are assigned appear sufficient, and the imaginary of powerlessness, which convinces them to renounce any greater ones to which they might aspire. 'For whatever man imagines he cannot do, he necessarily imagines; and he is so disposed by this imagination that he really cannot do what he imagines he cannot do.'[3] Here is the passionate mechanism, activated by the (social) imaginary of powerlessness, for converting assignation into self-assignation.

Conceived thus as distributive, domination appears as a compromise solution, reconciling the principal social contradiction of a desire that, on the one hand, seeks its own confirmation in the gaze of others – 'if we imagine that someone loves or desires . . . something we ourselves love or desire, . . . we shall thereby love or desire . . . it with greater constancy'[4] – and, on the other hand, attempts to keep others away from the very objects to which it has led them so successfully – 'and so we see that each of us, by his nature, wants the others to live according to his temperament; when all alike want this, they are alike an obstacle to one another, and . . . they hate one another.'[5] It follows that most of the opportunities for social joy are differential – to possess what others will not have – and the actions of *reserving* (to oneself, or to one's 'class') and *keeping away* (the others) are social domination's most characteristic gestures. But in order to be fully successful, the distributive operation of domination must meet an additional requirement; it must reserve certain objects of desire to the dominators, and make the dominated recognise them as desirable, *but with a decisive provision*: desirable in general, but not for them. Ordinary employees must be able to recognise the desirability of the

3   *Ethics*, III, Definition 28.
4   Ibid., III, 31.
5   Ibid., Scholium.

power to guide the company, but without making it an object of _their_ desire. They will thus remain riveted to the things that have been assigned to them by the division of labour, which the workings of the powerlessness imaginary converted into a division of desire. As Bourdieu repeatedly emphasised, the division of desire is a structure of arbitrary assignations traced against a background of anthropological non-differentiation for which Spinoza provides the underlying principle: 'all have one common nature.'[6] Hidden from the outset by the arbitrariness of social classifications that seize individuals from birth, this background has very few opportunities to manifest itself as such. That is why it is necessary to keep reiterating the fact of its existence, contradicted by all the spontaneous experiences of a social world whose arbitrariness is converted into necessity by the collective imagination. As Pascal reminds the son of the Duke of Luynes, 'the whole title by which you possess your property is not a title of nature, but of human establishment. Another turn of the imagination of those who made the laws would have rendered you poor.'[7] But perhaps one must return to Spinoza for the most radical reaffirmation of this fundamental anthropological equality, and for the hope of dissipating, as little as one can, the learned distinctions and phantasmagorical transfigurations whose incessant imaginary production forever tracks:

[they say,] 'the mob, if it is not frightened, inspires no little fear', and 'the populace is either a humble slave, or a haughty master', and 'it has no truth or judgment', etc. But all have one common nature. Only we are deceived by power and refinement. Whence it comes that when two do the same thing we say, 'this man may

---

6   _Political Treatise_, VII, 27.

7   Blaise Pascal, 'First Discourse', in 'Three Discourses on the Condition of the Great', trans. Samuel Webb, marxists.org.

do it with impunity, that man may not'; not because the deed, but because the doer is different. Haughtiness is a property of rulers. Men are haughty . . . But their arrogance is glossed over with importance, luxury, profusion, and a kind of harmony of vices, and a certain cultivated folly, and elegant villainy, so that vices, each of which looked at separately is foul and vile, because it is then most conspicuous, appear to the inexperienced and untaught honourable and becoming.[8]

Left to diffuse and impersonal mechanisms, the social division of desire, working through the mechanism set forth in *Ethics*, III, 49, makes individuals experience the arbitrariness of their assignations as necessity, as a *fatum* without a god, which there-fore deserves love, or at least less hatred than if one imagined it the result of a free cause. The great movement of imaginary social production assumes the task of providing justifications for the arbitrary made necessary. And from the time of the Greeks, these justifications have always fallen conspicuously inside the triangle of birth, wealth, and competence. With the eras of aristocratic and plutocratic legitimacy gone (at least in their pure forms), the contemporary mythogenesis of the university degree, as Bourdieu repeatedly insisted, struggles to hide its own indifference to content and its only true mission, which is to certify 'elites', namely, to provide alibis to the distri-bution of individuals within the social division of desire.

PASSIONATE EXPLOITATION

For all the deftness with which the business enterprise produces joy, rebaptised as 'consent', its engineering of desire remains too visible. Even those whose commitment is the most joyful know about the master-desire and are aware of the capture of their

---

8   *Political Treatise*, VII, 27.

efforts. Life under the master-desire is exploited life. But in what sense exactly is it exploited? Probably not in the way Marxian theory imagines it. For exploitation in the Marxist sense of the term only makes sense in conjunction with a substantialist labour theory of value, according to which exploitation is the name of the capitalist appropriation of surplus-value, measured by the difference between the total product and the value-equivalent assigned to the reproduction of labour-power – what is paid out in wages. The definition of the value of the labour-power that must be reproduced is however among the most uncertain, and is in fact circular: instead of the objectively and independently calculated value of the labour-power that must be reproduced *determining* wages, the wages themselves *indicate* the *actual* value reserved for the reproduction of labour-power. The chief problem however is that in order to follow the Marxian definition of exploitation, one must accept a substantialist theory of value whose substance is the duration of abstract labour.

As there are enough affinities and points of contact between Marx and Spinoza, there is no reason to pass over in silence what is probably (together with the dialectics of negativity and contradiction) their chief difference: value. Figure of transcendence surreptitiously reintroduced in immanence, substantial value is rejected by Spinoza in the same way he rejected everything that might serve to re-establish objective norms in relation to which fault and vice can be measured. Spinoza's philosophy is the affirmation of the absolute plenitude of the real and its perfect positivity, another reason why it scandalises: for it is not easy to hear that 'by reality and perfection I understand the same thing.'[9] One can however approach the Spinozist critique of substantial value from another side, notably that of the Scholium of *Ethics*, III, 9, which inverts the relation between

---

9   *Ethics*, II, Definition 6.

desire and value, positing – the exact opposite of our intuitive apprehension – that it is not desire which is attracted to a pre-existing and objectively determined value, but rather objects are constituted as valuable when desire invests them.[10] Value has nothing of substance contained in it; there are only the investments of desire and the ongoing axiogenesis that transfig-ures the desired into a *good*. This reversal holds for all values, aesthetic and moral as well as economic, however distant these domains of valorisation may seem from each other. (Durkheim, who took seriously the identity of the word, above and beyond the apparent heterogeneity of its usages, explicitly sought to develop a transversal theory of value.[11]) There can be no objec-tive value for Spinoza because complete immanence can only tolerate immanent norms. But the theoretically affirmed inex-istence of substantial value in no way precludes an account of the innumerable processes of valorisation. The values generated in these processes are no more than the products of composi-tion emerging from the interplay of investing powers, hence acts of *positing* and *affirmations* of value. There is no substantial value that could ground an objective norm and thus incontest-ably anchor arguments in disputes about distribution. There are only the temporary victories of certain powers that successfully imposed their valorising affirmations. Valuable is what the most powerful has declared as valuable. This however does not rule out the emergence of dissident valorisation communities in certain fields; indeed, struggles over valorisation constitute the everyday of the social life of value.

The same goes for the field of economic valorisation, which nothing, not even the apparent objectivity of numbers, can

---

10 'We neither strive for, nor will, neither want, nor desire anything because we judge it to be good; on the contrary, we judge something to be good because we strive for it, will it, want it, and desire it.' *Ethics*, III, 9, Scholium.

11 Émile Durkheim, 'Value Judgements and Judgments of Reality', in *Sociology and Philosophy*, Routledge, 2010.

ground in substantial norms. From this perspective, the Spinozist critique invites rather to reread the Marxian labour theory of value and surplus-value as an affirmation set against competing affirmations – and moreover as an involuntary homage that Marxian materialism pays to idealism by conceding implicitly that a theoretical elaboration ('an objective theory of value') provides the highest form of legitimacy when advancing a *demand*. And it is true that the norms of the *public sphere*, formal debating norms that require *generality* from arguments, keep subjecting political demands to the eternal question, 'By what right?' – 'By what right are you demanding? What grounds and justifies your demands?' The confusion that usually accompanies the reception of the Spinozist critique, read as the annihilation of all possible justifications since it annihilates any recourse to objective values, hence to 'general' principles, is entirely due to the acceptance of the convention of 'justification' (objectively illusory although no doubt socially necessary), to the point of having completely lost sight of the fundamentally groundless (and impossible to ground) character of all demands. To the question 'Why and by what right are you making this demand?' the answer is always *in the final analysis* 'Because': 'Because it's me'. It is by the natural right of my conatus and following its ingrained egocentricity, by the force of this desire of mine, that I make this demand; as for the rest, justification and 'general' arguments will be supplied as needed.[12] Expressing the profoundly affirmative nature of the conatus, demands are efforts of power [*puissance*], and their conflicts are decided, as all antagonistic encounters in the world are, by the elementary law of the stronger power – although evidently within the formal constraints on expressing one's power specific to the

---

12 On this subject, see Frédéric Lordon, 'La légitimité n'existe pas. Éléments pour une théorie des institutions', *Cahiers d'Économie Politique* 53 (2007).

social world, which can for example lead efforts of power to express themselves in a 'justified' discourse. That is why renouncing the Marxian theory of value, surplus-value, and exploitation is not at all grounds for abandoning the monetary debate and the conflict over distribution. Struggles over the distribution of money *exist*, and it is not necessary to invoke an objective and substantive theory of surplus-value in order to contest the division of value as unjust – assuming the constitutive partiality of the point of view that challenges the injustice. The ratio of income share distribution between the upper and lower deciles or centiles (inside the enterprise or in the whole economy), the rate of distribution of profits (i.e. dividends), or the part of the added-value captured by shareholders are all quantitative indicators that can validate the claim of injustice (in fact of discontent) by one of the parties in the conflict over distribution, a party that asserts its own norms by reference to other historical or geographical situations, or even by a pure, affirmative stance: 'The ratio between the ten highest and the ten lowest salaries in the enterprise should not exceed 20, or 10, or X. That's *our* norm, that's what *we say*.' But it is true that the convention of 'generality' and the obligation to justify, which call for buttressing demands with principles, are simultaneously the rags donned by affirmations of power *and* a formal elaboration that is no doubt indispensable to saving the whole society from the outbreak of violence that would otherwise follow the naked expression of demands in their original state of pure pronations.[13] The conventional expression of these pronations in the form of 'principles-talk' has therefore no intrinsic value, but the only – albeit vital – extrinsic value of serving as bulwark against pronatory chaos. This suggests that discursivity in the

---

13   Pronation is the posture of the hand, knuckles facing forward, in the motion of grabbing, a technical term used by the author to describe the naked attitude of the conatus as the gesture of grabbing something. See Lordon, *L'intérêt souverain*. [Trans.]

social world has less to do with truth than with, on the one hand, assaults by enterprises of power, and on the other hand, the social necessity of containing violence.

It is significant in any case that employees do not need to believe in the Marxian theory of surplus-value in order to feel exploited and engage in struggle. The idea of monetary injustice is not the only one at stake, even if it often provides these struggles with their main content. It is rather the more general idea of capture that transversely takes hold of the variety of these protests. But contrary to what one may think, the capture perspective, more than it helps to put the Marxian theory of surplus-value back in the saddle, suggests redefining – not abandoning – the idea of exploitation. At first sight this has all the markings of a paradox, since in the Marxian definition exploitation is precisely the capture of surplus-value by capital, which consists in depriving the employees of a part of the value *they* have produced. It is not however the dispossession from that part of value *in itself* that turns it into exploitation, but its *private appropriation* by the capitalist. Were the surplus-value handed over, not to the capitalist but to the enterprise under total internal democratic control of the employees, or more accurately to the employees collectively, who would still think of calling it 'exploitation'? Yet formally the employees would still be *personally* deprived of the surplus-value as the difference between the total value and the value of the reproduction of their labour-power. The 'objective' calculus of the labour theory of value, which supposedly entails a finding of exploitation, would be maintained, without however leading to that conclusion. Therefore, if exploitation there is, it falls under a political theory of capture more than under an economic theory of value. Since the Marxian theory of objective value was conceived, and its impasses tolerated, for the very purpose of supporting a concept of exploitation, the cost of renouncing it is less than imagined once that concept can be supported in another way.

Moving from the economics of surplus-value to the politics of capture requires specifying the nature of what is being captured. And to this there is an immediate Spinozist reply: the power of acting. The master-desire captures the power of acting of the enlistees. It makes the conative energies of others work in its service, others that social structures, for example those of the employment relation, have enabled it to mobilise in the service of *its* enterprise (let us recall that the word 'enterprise' designates the desiring action at its most general). In the worst case, the operative desire is the desire to avoid the evil of material destitution, and the power of acting is only surrendered in an environment of sad affects. In the best case, the specific epithumogenesis of the enterprise (this time in the capitalist sense) co-linearises the conatus of employees through affects of joy, but while riveting their power of acting to the division of desire, hence restricting its effectuation to extremely limited domains, and in this way dooming enlistees to fragmented contributions, which only the master-desire totalises. The capture by the master-desire – the powers of acting occupying themselves in its service – constitutes therefore a *dispossession of creative labour*, dispossession not only of the monetary value of the product of labour through the capture of surplus-value by capital, but more generally, because capture is what defines all forms of bossing, with the dispossession of *authorship* [*authorat*]. Helped by the social mechanisms of personalisation and institutional embodiment, bosses appropriate the symbolic profits of the collective creative labour of the enlistees, which they then attribute *in toto* to themselves. In all generality, the dispossession carried out by bossing is thus a form of recognition-capturing by the individual monopolisation of a fundamentally collective authorship: having hidden from view the work of all those who helped them, science bosses draw their recompense from being remembered for posterity as 'discoverers'; university mandarins sign their names to publications for which their assistants provided the statistics and documentation without which their arguments would fall apart; film directors win recognition as unique authors of sets of images that only their directors of photography were technically capable of producing, and so on.

This is not to deny the frequent inequality of contributions, an objectively hierarchical articulation where some have the character of 'bringing together' and others of 'being brought together'. There is clearly a difference between supplying the guiding idea and contributing to its realisation. The point is however to emphasise how almost all contributions are effaced, leaving a single one visible, and moreover in a manner that maintains the primal division, already stressed by Marx and Engels, between labour of 'conception' and labour of 'execution'. Should we then make a distinction between authors, who provide the guiding idea, and executors, whose work is irreducibly collective? Without the latter, the former would remain an absolutely dead letter, a purely private virtuality. The ambitions of authorship – another name for the master-desire – which, being too high, cannot be satisfied by the author alone, themselves lead to enlistment and to the division of labour that extends into a division of desire. To this must be added a division of recognition, which is also a division of joy. For the chances for joy are maximised at the top of the enlistment pyramid, that summit point where the enterprise (of whichever nature) recapitulates its collective doing and offers it in a finished and condensed form to the external gaze of the wider public, source of the highest recognition. Only the summit of the pyramid of each enterprise is known externally, that is, only those who occupy those summits and who, being dominant, take great care to reserve for themselves the chances for joy to which their position already objectively destined them, through all the mechanisms of embodiment-representation. The immense joy coming from the outside in the form of public recognition

falls to them first, and only or almost only to them. Once recognised and filled with joy, the master-desire turns to recognise
and bring joy to its closest enlistees, who then proceed to recognise theirs, and so forth along the hierarchical chains that are
the gutters of a *trickle-down economy* of joy.

The process of composing powers of acting that is eventually captured by bossing, whether in the monetary form or in
the symbolic form of recognition, is only made possible by the
assignations of the division of labour and the humble rewards
of the division of joys. Although cast in the particular social
structures of the capitalist employment relation, both are in fact
fundamental mechanisms of passionate life, incessantly
rearranging conative efforts and producing their alignment with
the direction of the master-desire. This subordinated alignment
is decidedly exploitative, since it subjugates powers of acting to
the enterprise of a single one (or several), but it is a passionate
exploitation. To say that people function by passion is no more
than to recognise the exclusive power of affects to guide the
energy of the conatus. That the capitalist boss captures a part of
value is so evident a fact that it would be absurd to contest it.
But the lack of an objective, substantial reference in which to
ground the measure of surplus-value obliges us to detach the
idea of exploitation from the calculation of value, and to define
it in another way. We should not however lament the impasse of
the Marxian solution to the problem of exploitation; it is rather
an opportunity – the opportunity to construct a concept of
exploitation that accounts for *bossing in general*. Even before
converting the product into money, the *capitalist* boss captures
the same thing as any other specific boss (the mandarin, the
crusader, the choreographer . . .). The primary object of capture
by the general boss is effort, namely, power of acting. But the
capture of enlisted conative energies through alignment with
the master-desire can only happen under passionate determination. That is then what the boss generally exploits: power and

passions, power properly guided by passions. The epithumo-genic work has no other function than to (partially) re-order the passionate life so as to facilitate exploitation and make it work in a suitable direction; all it does is to propose affects and induce appropriately oriented desires. Conatus and affects are the components of joyful auto-mobility, capital's source for the best conversion of labour-power into labour. Fundamentally, these are the resources that the capitalist bossing-class exploits, but as its own specific declension of bossing in general. Each specific bossing relation converts the effort of the powers of acting passionately composed around it into its specific objects of desire; the capitalist bossing rela-tion, into money; other bossing relations, into the type of recognition that is particular to their respective fields. But all reach their goals by the same mobilisation of conative ener-gies properly guided by affects. Led by an ambition that cannot be satisfied by their own means, they must all seek to lead on the enlistees in their direction.

For this is indeed the task of capitalist epithumogenesis, to pull the legs of the employees, in all the senses of that expres-sion. First, to get them to move, which means, returning to the basic significations of auto-mobility, to make them *move them-selves*, and in the most mundanely physical sense: by getting them to put one foot before the other, as revealed by the striking spectacle of the daily migration towards factories and business districts, those large concentrations of capitalist passionate exploitation on which waves of conatus-vectors converge, aligned up to their correlation within the physical space of an underground train carriage, a great current of co-linearised powers of acting heading for the master-desire. To pull the legs of employees is also to make them *function*, namely, to get them to occupy themselves in an appropriate manner, in keeping with the requisites of the valorisation of capital. In the first sense, employees must simply walk, that is, move themselves and advance. In the second sense, they must walk *well*, namely, *the right way*. But the meaning that is most telling of epithumo-genesis is perhaps the idiomatic one, when we say, after the scales have fallen from our eyes, 'You are leading me on, you led me on'. To make employees take the master-desire as their own is indeed to 'lead them on', to make them believe that when they occupy themselves on behalf of capture they are toiling for their own 'fulfilment', that their desire is truly where they find them-selves, that they have the devil's own luck since the pleasant comes bound up with the useful, their 'accomplishments' bound up with the necessities of material reproduction. All these oper-ations of imaginary affective induction constitute passionate exploitation. And when they are particularly successful, as the saying goes, the enlistees no longer walk – they run.

COMMUNISM OR TOTALITARIANISM (TOTALITARIANISM, THE HIGHEST STAGE OF CAPITALISM?)

The well co-linearised employees may very well run; yet they run a little sideways. The residue of the backdrop of threat and its sad affects persistently muddles the joyful affects of the best epithumogeneses, hanging over them as a confused but nagging awareness of the master-desire and its deliberate, targeted, intentional, and (above all) easy to identify and pinpoint affec-tive engineering. The crab walk will be their lot, first, because few will be able to cast themselves entirely and without the slightest reserve into the project of the full colonisation of their being proposed to them by the neoliberal enterprise. The heter-ogeneity with respect to the definitions one usually finds in philosophy or political science does not in any way prohibit from speaking about totalitarianism in the case of a project of the complete investment of individuals by an institution. Of course, the ideal of the totalitarian practice of the neoliberal makeover of souls is that it should be merely transitional, reaching as fast as possible its (oxymoronic) horizon of free wills permanently conforming ('consenting'), so that once the norm has been perfected and engrammed the normalising scaffolding can be withdrawn. The goal is reached when employees, 'moving entirely of their own accord' and without needing to be further co-linearised, strive in the organization's direction and bring it their power of acting unreservedly as a perfectly voluntary commitment.

But the effort remains irreducibly contradictory, doubly so in fact. First, it is contradictory from the side of the employees, who experience it at all the degrees of recalcitrance, from the feeling of being purely and simply bludgeoned into submission, up to a muddled awareness troubled by the always visible facts of epithumogenesis (intentionality, purpose, threat) – with the exception of course of those elite employees who invest in the enterprise as much as it invests in them. Then, it is also contradictory from the side of capital, in that much as 'obedient free will' may be a superior solution from the standpoint of the intensity of commitment, it remains afflicted by an irreducible uncertainty that only a belief in oxymora can overcome. For the 'free will' is ever capable of going back to the pursuit of its own ends, and there is nothing it hates as much as hierarchical subordination. That is why in the highest ranks of the employee-class, where the most 'autonomous' subjects are found, organisations take pains to make subordination feel, and sometimes really be, as light as possible, even dreaming of making it altogether forgotten.

Some in the form of a well-defined analysis, others in the form of premature prophesy or naive rapture, a good number of recent studies in the sociology of work discovered in the figure of the artist a pertinent metaphor, and even more than a metaphor, a common model, for those employees reputed to have personal qualities of strategic importance to their company, notably 'creativity'. Since neither the products nor the processes of creativity can be determined or controlled in advance, the only possible approach to the creative subject is one of 'laissez-faire'.[14] The mobilisation of these strategic employees thus assumes *by its essence* conditions of extensive autonomy and weak directionality. Yet this very rare, isolated tribe, this limit-point of employment, has been turned into a general model for the overall project of neoliberal normalisation. Is not the artist the very emblem of 'free will', and the unreserved commitment of the self? More to the point, is not the artist the proof par excellence that the second correlates with the first? For artistic productivity arises from the alliance between the artist's specific skills and the condition of coinciding with one's desire. And this is precisely the ideal formula which the neoliberal enterprise would like to reproduce on a large scale, evidently with the provision that each employee's 'own desire' must be aligned with the desire of the enterprise. But there comes a point when hier-archical relaxation, the better to give free rein to the creativity of the 'creatives', begins to contradict the very existence of the structure of capital. If in order to give the best of their talents these employees must be left to themselves, nothing can stop them from escaping should they find even the residual manage-rial supervision too onerous, and the appropriation of the fruits of their singular creativity too abusive. One may argue that these unconventional employees dispose of an uncommon bargaining power that allows them to sell their singularity at a high price, and stay on the better side of the market relation between the demand and the supply of labour. The fact remains that the existence of such scandalous biotopes of autonomy from the common law of employment is to some extent an homage vice pays to virtue, since by implicitly recognising the productive superiority of uncoerced labour, the enterprise comes close to

14   See especially Pierre-Michel Menger, *Portrait de l'artiste en travailleur. Métamorphoses du capitalisme*, Seuil, 2006.

repudiating itself as a hierarchical structure. If capital both reaches the conclusion that free autonomy is the most productive formula, and sees in this form of mobilisation of the power of acting, since it does away with the *reserve*, a model to generalise, then the limit-point of the artist-employee comes close to becoming a point of contradiction. Does not capitalism, in conceding that abolishing the hierarchy and giving free rein to initiative and collaboration are the real requisites of productive creativity, embark on the road to the free association of workers, impelled by its inherent tendency? If indeed the artist is a possible and desirable avatar of the worker, and from capital's own point of view, then the very idea of employment as a relation of hierarchical subordination is fundamentally called in question.

Quite surprised, at times even excited to discover this unexpected confluence of the worker and the artist, or, to a lesser extent, the rise of new forms of work that call for an expanded autonomy, some analyses have missed both the specific addenda of managerial discourse itself,[15] and the narrowness of the segment of employment that is actually concerned. But while it is important not to forget that the condition of the majority of employees remains subordinated and heteronomous, it is equally important to recognise this vanishing point of capitalism, but so as to grasp its paradoxical intensity and the tensions it can already produce in the present. For to imagine it realised, as a general model of productivity based on free creativity, brings back a dialectical figure we had believed lost: that of capitalism's self-transcendence out of its own contradictions – this time neither through the misalignment between the forces of production and the relations of production, with the transformation of workers into a proletarian mass in the factory itself producing the revolutionary force, nor through the endogenous

15   Luc Boltanski and Eve Chiapello, *The New Spirit of Capitalism*, Verso, 2007.

deformation of the organic composition of capital and the fall in the rate of profit. Rather, capitalism could put itself in danger unaided, by pursuing to the end a dream of productive mobilisation that contains at bottom the principle of its negation: the freedom to create, the freedom to collaborate and a recalcitrant attitude towards hierarchical management. What is more, such an attitude would necessarily determine the collective organisation of labour on a deliberative-democratic basis – in other words, communism realised!

Obviously, capitalism will not go that far, but it will persist in attempting the complete possession of souls. Employees will not all become artists, thus capable of escaping through the communist line of flight. For the pre-eminent among them, the extension of their latitude, considered by capital itself to be in keeping with its new productive requisites, implies a firm adherence to the work of co-linearisation. Thus this 'autonomy', which a superficial reading of managerial literature took somewhat too quickly at face-value, is in fact the mask of a new servitude. However dubious the value of establishing a hierarchy of loathsomeness in servitude, nothing prohibits calling the neoliberal project of the *possession* of souls totalitarian, since it is, in fact, total. Today's situation echoes the long-past slogan 'socialism' or 'barbarism': on the one hand the paradoxical ideal of the artist-employee escaping into the free association of workers, and on the other hand capital's demand for the total subordination of the desires and affects of its subjects. The two seem to usher the present situation toward a formally very similar bifurcation: communism or totalitarianism.

WELL THEN, (RE-)COMMUNISM!

Clarifying the alternatives facilitates the choice. As does returning to the *problem*. The point of departure was this: someone feels like doing something that requires the collaboration of several people. This community of action is *ipso facto* a political community, if we call political any situation in which there is a composition of powers of acting. Of course, it is quite possible to choose to reserve the term political to other things, as Rancière does for example with the eruption of those without a part into the whole;[16] but here we will apply our definition. The question is then that of the constitution of this enterprising political community, both in the genetic sense of the mechanisms through which the community arrives at constituting itself, and in the 'constitutional' sense of the formal arrangements that govern its functioning once assembled. What are the desirable relations for the constitution of an enterprise conceived very generally as a convergence of powers of acting?

The constitution of enterprising capitalist communities have had, so far, all the structures of the employment relation and the monetary economy with a division of labour in its favour. The question of how individuals enter into it is resolved rather simply: primarily under the effect of material necessity – not because they spontaneously want to join. How will the lives of the enlistees in the enterprise turn out, will they be sad or joyful? That will be decided by the vicissitudes of the process of epithumogenesis. Under what political constitution? The answer is in keeping with the egocentricity of the master-desire: hierarchical and monarchical. Assisted by all the structures of capitalist enlistment that affirm its right to capture, the master-desire views enlistment into its cause as self-evident and fails to even notice anymore its inability to pursue the enterprise, which exceeds its means of power, without the contributions of other powers that it variously obtains. For how many capitalist enterprises would remain if people were freed from material necessity? Suspending the necessity clause will not eliminate all

---

16 Jacques Rancière, *Disagreement: Politics and Philosophy*, University of Minnesota Press, 2004.

enterprising communities (in general). It even has the virtue of helping to imagine the enterprise in the canonical form of the *association*, free from its main distortion, the bossing distortion. 'One' wishes to do something that requires the involvement of others, and must therefore convince them to join, other than by the 'arguments' of material dependence. Since passionate servitude is universal, this form of gathering is as much subject to it as any other. What changes is the nature of the determinations that result in compositions of powers. Associates lose at least a part of their status as enlistees, since they join a proposition of desire in which they recognise their own desire as it has already been determined before, and *otherwise* – namely, neither under the requisites-threats of material reproduction, nor deliberately induced by a master-desire.

The communist answer to the general question of the enterprise begins therefore thus: if people want to do something together, they must do it under an egalitarian political form. Political is the quality of any situation in which there is interaction between or composition of powers. Hence the communist position could be generically defined by the idea that in any situation that qualifies as political, equality must prevail in principle. In principle does not however mean absolutely, since it is certain that individuals are not equal in power with respect to the realisation of things. A playwright presents an extraordinary text. Who would deny that such a contribution is not of the same nature as that of the electrician or the wardrobe supervisor? Who would contest the playwright's power as authentically creative? Yet there must be electricians and wardrobe supervisors for the show to take place, and for the text of genius to reach the public. The problem is never posed in these terms, because the employment relation's 'immediate' solution of providing hired hands eventually leads to forgetting that it is a problem. To recover its sense requires a thought experiment that consists in imagining what political arrangements would need to take shape for the collective enterprise to be launched, *once the structures of the employment relation have been removed.* It is a fictional hypothesis, but one that provides a framework for thinking out both the problem of the (collective) enterprise at its most general, and the possibility of its non-capitalist solutions. The question arises in a particularly acute manner whenever the enterprise is founded in response to the initial proposition of one person. This proposition may be inherently strong enough to preclude any contestation of its hierarchically superior character. Yet some way must be found to bring other powers to it, since without their participation it would remain literally a fancy. It would be intellectual folly to put the text of *Richard III* on the same level as its costumes. Yet the costumes are necessary if the performance is to take place. There must be then a way to *bring* the wardrobe supervisor to it.

In the absence of the compulsion to enlist inherent in employment, the contributions of third parties to the singular proposition which they join represent from the outset a recognition that the proposition possesses a creative character to some degree, and this solely by virtue of the temporal sequence by which it was *first* put forward, and *then* it demonstrated enough force of attraction for others to have the desire to join it. This manner of constituting an enterprise nonetheless preserves an asymmetrical character, inscribed in a kind of contributive hierarchy that gives an eminence of fact to the initial proposition, which is also recognised as such by the other contributors by virtue of its very anteriority and the ulteriority of their own contributive engagement. If the communist idea is essentially about equality, the question then is how to understand the nature of an equality that accompanies a substantial, recognised inequality among contributors, and does not deny the asymmetry of those situations where the force of an initial proposition objectively gives the other contributions an *auxiliary* character. One formulation of what we might call the communist equation

could therefore be as follows: what form of equality can be realised under the legacy of the division of labour – and notably
under the most onerous of its legacies, to wit, the primary separation between 'conception' and 'execution'?

The solution to this equation must be sought under a
double constraint. On the one hand, the division of labour has
deepened to the point that it became the central fact (and also
the blind spot) of an entire desiring ethos, that is, a manner of
developing ambitions that 'spontaneously', and without even
being aware of it, assumes that others are prepared to be mobilised. In the division of labour duplicated in a division of desire,
it is wholly 'natural' that those who are best positioned should
desire in excess of their means, confident in the knowledge that
others will join them, their contributions guaranteed to them
by the division of labour and the employment relation, and
therefore taken as both a habit and a certainty. On the other
hand, the division of labour supports this habit with its full
apparatus of social relations and the full history of that apparatus, namely, the inertia of its assignations, and primarily those
granting to some the role of 'conception' and reserving to
others that of 'execution.' For these repeated assignations have
real effects: effects of empowerment for some, to whom the
division of labour brings all the conveniences of its specialised
means that are so many resources for the deployment of their
power; effects of disempowerment for others, who are inca-
pacitated and who incapacitate themselves according to the
passionate (and social) mechanism by which a person 'really
cannot do what he imagines he cannot do'. And so the respective positions of playwright and electrician always fall to the
same people.

If the full solution of the communist equation consists in a
restructuring of the division of labour in a way that would
redistribute the chances of conception – and symmetrically the
tasks of execution (assisted no doubt by the development of

new technologies) – no one articulated its horizon, Spinozist as much as Marxist, as well as Étienne Balibar: 'as many as possible, thinking as much as possible.'[17] But what to do with the idea of equality during the long transition, under the persistent constraint of the division of labour and the unequal distribution of the work of conception and execution, save for the miraculous emancipations of certain 'proletarian nights',[18] or the minor local victories that gradually facilitate the rescue of certain individuals from the specialisations to which the division of labour had riveted them, so that the electrician might increasingly come to have opinions about the staging? While the unequal social division of desire still resists the realisation of substantive equality in the contributive order of concrete activity with the full force of its inertia, it does not however prevent the rapid implementation of egalitarian politics in the form of a deliberative politics of enterprise, namely, as equal participation in the determination of a shared collective destiny. Under the effect of the legacy of the division of labour, its differential empowerments, its imprisoning specialisations, and its unequal authorisations, the horizon of contributive de-hierarchisation is no doubt doomed to remain distant. Yet individuals can become equal very quickly, as far as collective reflexivity is concerned, namely, as full partners in a common destiny of doing.

It is the recurrent task of an appropriate constitution to tend towards this form of equality. With a wordplay that will hopefully have some inducing effect, we can call the general

17   Étienne Balibar, *Spinoza and Politics*, Verso, 2008, p. 98.

18   A reference to the original title of Jacques Rancière's book, in which he rereads working-class archives of the nineteenth century and reports the experience of those workers who appropriated for themselves the practices of literary and poetic writing and the high culture from which all social mechanisms worked to exclude them. See Rancière, *The Nights of Labor: The Workers' Dream in Nineteenth-Century France*, trans. John Drury, Temple University Press, 1989.

enterprise (and the productive enterprise in particular) re-commune,[19] *res communa* modelled after *res publica*, a thing that is merely common, since it is narrower in number and purposes than the public thing, but is an enclave of shared life and can be organised as such according to the same principle as the ideal republic: radical democracy. While it is clear what gulf separates the ideal republic from the real one, at least within 'republican' political systems the words have been spoken, at the peril of those who, while generally ready to back a system committed to systematically mock it, crow over the idea of democracy without taking into consideration that one day they may be *taken seriously*. In any case, to play on the shared root of the words republic and recommune is to suggest, against an inconsistency on which capitalism's hopes for survival hang, that the principle of radical democracy applies universally to any enterprise conceived as the co-existence and convergence of powers, hence independently of its purpose. Specifically, there are no grounds for exempting the industrial production of goods from this constitutional form. Since members place a part of their lives in common in an enterprise, they can only escape the enlistment relation, two-tiered by its nature as a monarchical constitution (the *imperium* of the master-desire), by sharing not only the enterprise's goal but also the complete command over the conditions of its collective pursuit, and ulti-mately by asserting their indisputable right to be full partners in what *concerns them*: what should the (productive) enterprise manufacture, in what quantities, at what pace, with what size of workforce and what structures of remuneration; what scale should it use for the reallocation of surplus, how should it adapt to changes in its environment? As all these questions have common consequences, none can in principle escape

---

19   Frédéric Lordon, *La crise de trop. Reconstruction d'un monde failli*, Fayard, 2009.

deliberation in common. Thus, the very simple recommunist principle is that what affects everyone should be everyone's thing – the very word recommune says it! It should be debted by everyone constitutionally and on equal terms.

In the beginning it was necessary to generalise the term 'enterprise' in order to make visible, beyond the particular case of the capitalist business enterprise – its general desiring nature, and the question of the relations between the desires that it cannot fail to elicit each time it becomes collective. But capitalism has so deeply permeated the word 'enterprise' that the latter has become its most characteristic (ideological) marker – go find the boss who would rather be called a 'capitalist' than an 'entrepreneur'. Under these conditions – fine! We shall give them back their 'enterprise' – but in order to make it right away the name of the thing that must be done away with. No (general) enterprise should ever again be configured like a (capitalist) enterprise – especially not the capitalist enterprises. And to help the general enterprise forget the capitalist enterprise once and for all, let us reserve to it for example the name that corresponds to its new organising principle: recommune. If the employment relation designates the relation of enlistment by which individuals are determined to bring their power of acting to a master-desire in exchange for money, and at the price of being dispossessed of any ability to participate in running (their) business, then the recommune realises its abolition pure and simple.

But the recommune does not exhaust the communist idea. For the question of the recommune-enterprise remains *local*. Beyond its borders the question of the market remains, and consequently also that of the division of labour. Should the definition and coordination of economic activities at the macro-social level be left to the market or organised by planning, and if the latter, by what kind of planning (partial or total, central or delegated-hierarchical, etc.)? Finally, the recommune leaves unanswered, or rather without any *new* answer, the problem of work. If it liberates its members from the monarchy of the master-desire, it does not liberate them from work as the form of activity that is ever more absorbed in the aims of material reproduction, and especially in those of the valorisation of capital. We owe a particular debt to Antoine Artous[20] and Moishe Postone[21] for having recovered in Marx's thought that which Marxist commentaries (not to mention the 'actually existing socialisms') forgot about, to wit, the goal of the radical liberation of work, understood as a genitive objective: the liberation of people *from* work, and the (re)separation between *work* and *activity*. Against all essentialisations-anthropologisations that have entirely confused the first with the second and made work a kind of universal of the human condition – as Hannah Arendt notably did – these readings have the virtue of recalling, both Marx's attempt to historicise his own categories (and those of political economy) by making work, rigorously conceptualised, the distinctive invention of capitalism,[22] and, in the same gesture, the fact that 'work' could never absorb all the possibilities of (social) effectuations open to individual powers of acting. Finally, these readings explicitly put the transcendence of work, to the full extent possible, at the horizon of communism, a horizon that cannot, it is worth mentioning, be enclosed in a list, a plan, or a defined programme: 'Communism is for us not a *state of affairs* which is to be established, an *ideal* to which reality will have to adjust itself. We call communism the *real* movement which abolishes the present state of things.'[23]

---

20   Antoine Artous, *Travail et émancipation sociale. Marx et le travail*, Éditions Syllepse, 2003.

21   Moishe Postone, *Time, Labor, and Social Domination: A Reinterpretation of Marx's Critical Theory*, Cambridge University Press, 1996.

22   Artous, *Travail*, Chapters 1–3.

23   Marx and Engels, 'The German Ideology', p. 57.

SEDITIOUS PASSIONS

But whence would this 'real' movement emerge, if the point of departure is the idea that the free and autonomous will is a fiction? To be generous, was not this idea at least useful for making liberation thinkable, and keeping the hope for it alive? Of all the misinterpretations that afflict the philosophical position of determinism, the most characteristic is perhaps the claim that it is unable to account for change, 'since everything is preordained'. What surprises can history hold in store for us in a world where all sequences of events are necessary? Is not determinism the eternal repetition of the same, and, by definition, the exclusion of the 'new'?

Everything is false in these verdicts of impossibility. We should first take a moment to show in what way (Spinoza's) determinism is not a fatalism, the script of the ineluctable set for all eternity, and how – without conceding anything – it by no means entails that the complete future of the universe is already known. For the supposedly critical encounter between determinism and novelty serves above all to expose the pretensions of the various metaphysics of subjectivity, and the social sciences that rely on them to make the heroic rebounds of the free will the sole motor, the condition *sine qua non*, of major historical transformations. To make a revolution is to shake off the yoke; therefore, one must have had the will to break one's chains, and this will could only have been a great moment of 'freedom'. Those who breathlessly clamour for the anti-capitalist uprising, calling for a liberation understood as emancipation from the servitudes of the social order, and potentially as – using the language of rupture – total liberation, namely, the reaffirmation of the sovereign autonomy of the subjects who regain the free command of their lives, are unaware of the deep intellectual kinship that binds them to the liberal thought they imagine themselves fighting, and of which their orations are almost as canonical an expression as the entrepreneurs' apologies. For the entrepreneurs too are free, masters of their success, at times even engaged in storming the Bastilles (the monopolies that want to corner the market, the restrictions on competition that dissuade from risk-taking); in short, they are equally busy 'changing the world' – in their own way. The 'innovators' of both kinds, revolutionaries of the social order or of the industrial order, are united above all in their common loathing of deterministic thought, to them an offence against their freedom, which in the last analysis is the sense they have of their unique ability to transform the world. The only difference between the two is the nature of the transformations sought by these otherwise equally liberal subjects. Witness the gesture of revulsion unfailingly and almost universally provoked by any suggestion that we may not be the free beings we like to imagine ourselves as. The purest formula of disgust is perhaps the one offered by Schelling, for whom to be conditioned was to be reduced to the rank of things – that by which 'anything becomes a thing'.[24] This gesture of revulsion indicates the depth of the roots of a scheme of thought shared by agents who believe themselves to differ politically in everything, whereas philosophically they differ in nothing (in any case, nothing *fundamental*).

The category of the 'new' is perhaps the site par excellence where all these confusions and common grounds are concentrated. For the new is the counterpart, in the world of objective things, of freedom in the world of subjective actions, and thus would like to pass for a kind of uncaused advent, an ineffable event that is an absolute exception to all known laws; a dazzling manifestation of freedom's ability to break with the past as the ability to suspend *absolutely* the order of the world and make it

---

24   F. W. J. Schelling, 'Du Moi comme principe de la philosophie', in *Premiers écrits*, PUF, 1987. Cited in Franck Fischbach, *Sans objet. Capitalisme, subjectivité, aliénation*, Vrin, 2009, p. 67.

bifurcate. In other words, coming from these false non-believers, it is exactly what is called a *miracle*. How can an event come about in a way that escapes the sequence of causes and effects, namely, out of nowhere? And, conversely, how to maintain the radicality of a 'new' that can be derived from a causal unfolding, rightfully knowable? Perhaps the only way we can avoid this dilemma is by downgrading the idea of the new, for example by reducing it to the finite abilities of the human understanding that sets itself to judge it. 'New' is nothing more than the name for what lies outside our ordinary experience, the quality we ascribe to what surprises us. But to surprise human understanding – to exceed its simple limits – should not in principle suffice to ground a metaphysical verdict. That the infinite complexity, synchronic as well as diachronic, of the concatenation of causes and effects eludes the human mind is a lacuna inscribed in the mind's very nature as finite mode, but not a sufficient reason to occasionally declare the concatenating order suspended. For to the infinite understanding, that of God or one of his lieutenants such as Laplace's demon, there are no 'surprises' and nothing that can lead to declaring an exception to the causal sequence. The 'new' cannot be new, at least with respect to the radicality that it assumes, because of the unfailing universality of the causal production of things, and finally because of the infinite understanding that loses sight of nothing of that production. It is only our understanding that lacks a clear grasp of things and wonders at everything that eludes it, calling it freedom/novelty – at least when it relates to history. It is true that airplanes hurtling into towers, or the fall, almost from one day to the next, of a curtain said to be of iron, catches us unprepared. But can our astonishment be the gauge of a subsequent metaphysical postulate, just because of our initial inability to perceive the 'event's' lengthy incubation? It can only be such a gauge because it fits perfectly with the ideas people like to have – especially people of the neoliberal era – of their own 'creative freedom' and *inaugural* power, namely, of their capacity for unconditioned action.

It is indeed because it insists on pleading its own defence that liberal freedom struggles to see 'novelty' where one could simply speak of change. For, obviously, nothing holds in the discourse of free will when it tries to pass for the sole guarantor of political transformations (against the 'resignation' of determinism), maintaining that because something represents a change relative to the old, it must be 'logically' new, and that only free wills could have first willed that change and then brought it into being. But the sequence of causes and effects is in principle fully compatible with change. Stars die that once shone; the earth that was calm suddenly opens up; hills that used to be part of the landscape collapse in an earthquake – and are *no longer* there. None of this, which can only be called 'change', is an exception to the laws of determinism, or requires the disruptive intervention of a freedom (but perhaps the defenders of novelty intend to appeal to the will of God). The same is true in the historical and social world, whose phenomena of both reproduction and transformation are likewise *produced*, namely, determined to occur by some or other causal sequence, even though, unlike dying stars and sliding hills, these sequences are the product of human action. For these actions are no less caused. And these causal sequences have no other motors than the conative energies and passions that steer them. Collective human life reproduces itself, or begins to change, solely as a consequence of the interplay of people's inter-affections, or, to say this in the simplest way possible, out of the effect they have on one another, but always through the mediation of institutions and social relations. The starting point is understanding in what way institutions can be seen as collective affective devices,[25]

---

25   On this see Lordon, 'L'empire des institutions' and 'La puissance des institutions'.

namely, as social things endowed with the power to affect multitudes in order to make them live in accordance with certain relations; that indeed is exactly what the disentangling of the passions of the employment relation revealed. However, the passions that work to keep individuals subordinate to institutional relations can also, at times, reconfigure themselves to work against those same relations. In keeping with the principle of causality, they do not reconfigure themselves of their own accord, but always under the effect of a prior affection, often that last straw which institutional power [*pouvoir*] failed to contain and that will cause its downfall by setting the multitude back into motion. Spinoza calls this affect, generically, 'indignation'. It is not a moral but an eminently political affect, which drives the subjects (*subditus*) to unite in revolt in the wake of an offence, perpetrated as it may be against only one of them, but which they experience as concerning them all. This general contagion of the sadness inflicted on a single one causes the marginal overflowing of common sadness that determines a common reactive movement of enlisted conatus, in keeping with the mechanism that stipulates that 'the greater the sadness, the greater is the part of a man's power of acting with which the man will strive to remove the sadness'.[26] As with the sailors of the battleship Potemkin swinging into mutiny, indignant at the death penalty imposed on those whose only crime was to protest against rotten meat, an abusive suspension can trigger an uprising in a factory, or one lay-off too many end up sending the managers into the street. The link between causes and effects does not operate differently in these exceptional moments. It simply no longer works at reproduction, but rather at making the course of things bifurcate, thus producing change.

---

26 *Ethics*, III, 37, Demonstration.

BECOMING PERPENDICULAR

> GAY: *Better than wages, ain't it?*
> PERCE: *Oh, anything's better than wages.*
>
> John Houston, Arthur Miller, *The Misfits*

Thus there is no need to appeal to any free will hypothesis in order to account for moments of abrupt change. They owe everything to the determinism of passionate dynamics – in this case angry passions, the best, or the least bad, of the sad passions. When the indignation that gets people moving prevails over the *obsequium* that makes them stay put, a new affective vector is formed, and individuals who used to be determined to respect institutional norms (for example, those of the employment relation) are suddenly determined to sedition. People do not however cease to be determined, even for a moment, when they cross their threshold of anger. The only difference is that they are now determined to do *something else*. What external conditions will this movement encounter, what future and what effect will they promise to it? This is yet another matter, but no less graspable in the last analysis within the perspective of passionate dynamics (and their institutional mediations). Will the eruption of indignation remain isolated, and fail to affect anyone beyond those immediately concerned? Or will it encounter a larger process of affective crystallisation, upon which, as small as it originally was, it will produce effects of catalysing precipitation, as in the Lip factory in 1973, where authorities feared that a local, seditious attempt at self-management might 'spread a syphilis through society' – in the words of the then minister of the economy Valéry Giscard d'Estaing, according to his colleague at the ministry of industry, Jean Charbonnel.[27]

---

27   See Christian Rouaud, *Les Lip. L'imagination au pouvoir*, DVD, Les Films du Paradoxe, 2007.

Indeed, indignation sometimes spreads like syphilis. It overturns the affective equilibria that have until then determined the subjects to submit to institutional relations, and leads them to desire to live, not according to their free will, but *as it pleases them – ex suo ingenio* – which implies, not some miraculous leap into the unconditioned, but a step into a life *determined in another way*. Moreover, quite often what pleases is recomposed collectively: the sailors of the Potemkin seize power and exercise it; the employees of Lip experiment with democratic self-management; in every case, new relations are invented. Because he made himself odious, but through one of those marginal abuses that pushed things beyond a critical threshold, the general boss, against his will, converted the affects of fear into affects of hate, and himself pushed the enlistees to de-linearise. Indignation is the generic name of the passionate dynamics that suddenly reopens the angle α and disaligns the conatus-vector d from the master-vector D (Figure 2.1). If the aim of enlistment was $\alpha = 0$ and perfect co-linearisation, sedition restores the right angle. This geometry of (de-)capture inverts the meaning of the expression 'to restore to the set square', which usually signifies to conform to the norm (etymologically, the set square is the *norma*). The result of α becoming a right angle is that $\cos \alpha = 0$, and the conatus-vectors of the enlistees no longer allow anything to be captured (the capture product is $\vec{d} . \vec{D} = |\vec{d}| x |\vec{D}|$ x $\cos \alpha$, and because α is now a right angle, the result is 0). Sedition is thus becoming-orthogonal, taking the perpendicular and not the tangent. Orthogonality is perfect disalignment, which may be a prelude to another realignment, this time negative, namely, openly antagonistic, on the same axis but in the opposite direction. An antagonistic alignment works not only to escape capture but to destroy the capturer, or at least diminish the capturer's effect. For when $\alpha = 180°$, $\cos \alpha = -1$, and not only the master-desire $\vec{D}$ no longer draws any benefit from $\vec{d}$, but $\vec{d}$ takes $\vec{D}$'s traction away from it

(Figure 2.2). However, while they await open war, the unsubdued are perpendicular. Passionate exploitation proceeded by co-linearisation and consisted in the hijacking and diversion [*détournement*] of powers of acting. The perpendicular revert back from that diversion. Becoming-orthogonal is resisting the hijacking by the invention and affirmation of new objects of desire, new directions in which to strive, different from those obstinately indicated by $\vec{D}$, and no longer dictated by it.

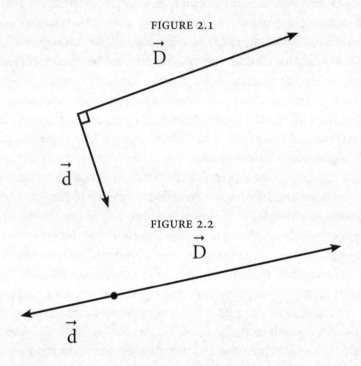

FIGURE 2.1

$\vec{D}$

$\vec{d}$

FIGURE 2.2

$\vec{D}$

$\vec{d}$

DE-FIXATION (A CRITIQUE OF [DIS-]ALIENATION)

At issue here is neither to restore nor to recover anything, especially not an originary freedom or a pure autonomy that only exists in the arguments of liberal individualism. It is true that, as interesting as they may be, contemporary rereadings of the young Marx, keen on reviving his concept of alienation, while not necessarily falling into subjectivist apologetics almost inevitably return to schemas of loss and separation, and thus to imagining emancipation in the form of a *reunion*. Thus, individuals are alienated when they are 'cut off from their power of acting', and the ultimate meaning of disalienation is to find one's way 'back', so as to coincide with it again. As Pascal Sévérac has shown, not even Deleuze escapes this tendency in his own reading of Spinoza, when he makes the full 're-appropriation of one's power' the very meaning of ethical liberation.[28] Yet as Sévérac insists, this scheme of separation contradicts one of the most central tenets of Spinoza's philosophy to which Deleuze is otherwise so sensitive: immanence, which is absolutely opposed to the Aristotelian distinction between 'potentiality' and 'actuality'. For Spinoza there is no power that is not immediately and fully actual. In other terms, there is no reserve in the Spinozist ontology. There is no unfulfilled or uneffectuated power that stands back, available for activation. Even when it can do very little, the conatus is always exhausting what it can do.[29] François Zourabichvili is quite right to call attention to the existence of a Spinoza-speak.[30] This new language uses not only its own vocabulary, for example by renaming the affects, but also its own grammar, notably a conjugation system in which the past conditional does not exist. 'I could have ...' is the Spinozist non-sense par excellence, the tense of regret, which exists only as a chimera of the imagination, a retrospective illusion. For the conatus always saturates its 'possibilities' (to speak in this way is still inadequate). And no, it could not have been 'able' to, for to be able to do and to do are one and the same thing: we could

---

28 Sévérac, *Le devenir actif chez Spinoza*; see also his 'Le devenir actif du corps affectif', *Astérion* 3 (September 2005), asterion.revues.org.

29 It would be inaccurate to say that it 'becomes the full extent of what it can,' as that would suggest a movement from a weak or zero degree of achievement to full achievement.

30 Zourabichvili, *Spinoza*.

only have done what we did, neither more nor less. Why does Spinoza embark on such a difficult path, at the risk of an incomprehension that culminates with his assimilation between reality and perfection – 'by reality and perfection I understand the same thing', states with perfect brutality the Sixth Definition of *Ethics* II? In order to hold on to immanence to the end. Complete immanence requires that there should be no reserve, that the act should always coincide fully with power, otherwise the gap opened by what has not been accomplished will inevitably reintroduce the fault, the lack, the vice, thus bringing back the obverse figure of the norm, and with it, ultimately, transcendence, which unfailingly leads back to the God-King with whom Spinoza wants to break absolutely.

Thus even when they live under the regime of the most tyrannical of master-desires, individuals are not 'separated' from their power. They are merely determined to effectuate it in a particular direction, sometimes with sadness, when the master-desire is satisfied with ruling by fear, but sometimes also with joy, when the work of epithumogenesis has been successful. There is nothing to 'regain' that is not there already, for how could individuals lose or be separated from their power when that power is their very being?[31] This does not mean that one cannot speak of more or less in relation to power. There are certainly variations in power, which is precisely how the affects are defined, joy as an increase of power, and sadness as its diminution. But if that is the case, one can ask whether the joyful enlistees have anything to complain about, since, being joyful, their powers are increasing, and in what sense they can be said to be victims of alienation. In none, evidently, if by alienation we mean the loss of one's autonomy as subject; that autonomy does not exist, and passionate servitude is ubiquitous. Neither

---

31   'The striving by which each thing strives to persevere in its being is nothing but the actual essence of the thing.' *Ethics*, III, 7.

does one gain much from understanding alienation through the mysterious figure of the loss of or separation from one's powers. Significantly more, however, if we take it to mean *the contraction of the scope of one's effectuations*. The very important conceptual operation that Pascal Sévérac puts at the centre of his reading of Spinoza consists therefore in preparing the ground for abandoning the schemes of loss and separation (as well as those, conversely, of reunion and 're-coincidence' with oneself), in order to place in their stead the scheme of *fixation*. Although the capitalist employment relation separates individuals from the means and above all the products of production, passionate exploitation does not separate them from their own power, and we must stop thinking about liberation as that wonderful operation that would return it to them. However, while it does not separate them from it, passionate exploitation *fixes* the power of individuals to an extraordinarily limited number of objects – those assigned by the master-desire. If the concept of alienation is worth rescuing, it would be for the sake of giving it the meaning of 'the stubborn affect'[32] and 'the occupation of the mind'[33] – the condition of the mind filled with too few things, but completely so, thus impeded from expanding comfortably. It is in this sense that employees riveted to 'their' one activity-object, be it joyfully, are 'alienated', no differently than the cocaine addict, whose mind is entirely filled by images of white powder.

The entire conceptual shift proposed by Sévérac's reading consists in noting a symmetry too often missed in Spinoza's definition of the power of acting as the power of affecting *and being affected*.[34] It is the connotation of passivity that is part of

---

32   'The force of any passion, or affect, can surpass the other actions, or power, of a man, so that the affect stubbornly clings to the man.' *Ethics*, IV, 6.

33   Sévérac, *Le devenir actif chez Spinoza*, Chapter 4, 'Une théorie de l'occupation de l'esprit'.

34   *Ethics*, IV, 38.

the idea of 'being affected' that has obviously long obscured this symmetry in the concept of power, intuitively understood as solely the power to affect. It follows that it is part of power, and by right, to have made oneself sensitive to a great variety of affections, and to have opened wide the field of one's affectabilities. We could mention in this context the scholium on diet, in which Spinoza recommends supplying the body with all the varied elements that correspond to the complexity of its structure: tasty food, naturally, but also pleasant scents, melodious sounds, a variety of visual pleasures, etc.[35] Alienation is fixation: indigent enticements of the body, narrow confines of the things one can desire, a severely restricted repertoire of joys, obsessions and possessions that tie one's power to a single place and impede its expansion. One can count in this matter on the subjugating effects of the master-desire that aligns the enlistee in a single direction – its own – and would like to imprison everyone in its fixed idea. That is what alienation is, not loss, but closure and contraction. And becoming-orthogonal means re-widening the scope of desire by beginning to de-fixate.

HISTORY AS DISCONTENT (THE BLURRING AND RECONFIGURATION OF THE LANDSCAPE OF CLASS)

One can take the perpendicular alone, leaving society (or that part of society one no longer cares for) behind, as it used to be and as it remains. But only a collective becoming-orthogonal is capable of reshaping it. Whence, however, will the mass perpendicular arise, and what can set the history of capitalism back in motion? For traditional Marxism, the answer was the clash between capital and labour. But what remains of this vision? Certainly not nothing at all! Scenes like the one captured by

---

35   Ibid., IV, 45, Corollary 2, Scholium.

writer François Ruffin violently remind us of that.[36] When the workers of an LVMH sub-contractor, threatened by relocation, descend on the outsourcing company's general assembly and physically confront management as it presents to shareholders about the returns on their equity, their dividends, and the fabulous trend in the stock price, what we are invited to witness is an almost pure Marxian scene. Surprisingly, however, such scenes are rarer and rarer, even as neoliberal capitalism seems to us to be degenerating rapidly towards its original brutalities. But while in many respects this regression towards the pure form of its origins is very real, in others the social landscape of capitalism has profoundly mutated. From the moment when, despite being 'capital's men', top executives became employees, the original Marxian theory was in trouble. And this trouble kept on growing with what could be called the rise of management: the growing number of employees who partially crossed over symbolically to the 'side of capital'.[37]

What could it mean to 'symbolically cross over to the side of capital', when materially one does not in fact belong to the side of capital, other than that the affective composition of the individuals in question shifted largely to the joyful end of the scale, and they found themselves enthusiastically bringing their power of acting to the enterprise, that is, ultimately, aligning it with the desire of capital? Marxism's trouble is aggravated by the fact that this crossing is not an all-or-nothing affair, but a matter of degrees that can be laid out in a continuum, going from the lowest – the sullen employee who does the least, and reluctantly – to the highest – those who, albeit instrumentally, devote the totality of their working life, at times their whole life, to the success of the enterprise. The landscape of class is

36 François Ruffin, *La guerre des classes*, Fayard, 2008.
37 A term borrowed from Duménil and Lévy, *Économie marxiste du capitalisme*.

therefore the double of the passionate landscape of employment, and fully reflects the history of its affective enrichments. It has lost the simplicities of its beginnings, and is blurred by the employment relation's gradient of commitment, which in the final analysis is an affective gradient, a gradient of the employee's joy (or sadness) at living the life of an employee. This is where Spinoza meets Marx – and changes him, for the transformation can be described synthetically by borrowing from the lexicons of both: to 'symbolically cross over to the side of capital' is to have a joyful 'real subsumption'.

What then remains of the straightforward demarcations of the old class antagonism? Is it possible to discount as negligible the individuals' lived experience of commitment, arguing that it is no more than a 'subjective' superficiality where only objective material conditions should count? Certainly not, since, despite being individually experienced, there is nothing subjective about affects. They are objectively caused and they produce the movements of the conatus just as objectively. It was precisely Spinoza's aim to treat them 'as properties, just as pertinent [to human nature], as are heat, cold, storm, thunder, and the like to the nature of the atmosphere, which phenomena, though inconvenient, are yet necessary, and have fixed causes'.[38] Since the employee's subjective relationship to the employment situation is produced objectively, the employed condition *in itself* – the brute fact of the sale of labour-power to a capitalist employer – does not exhaust the objective content of employment life, as the limit case of the salaried CEO proves *ad absurdum*.[39] There is however no *break in continuity* between ordinary cases and this boundary case.

However deep it is, this blurring of the original landscape of

---

38   *Political Treatise*, I, 4.
39   This without taking into account more recent developments that actually tend toward 'de-waging' bosses by raising the elements of financial fortune (stock-options) in remuneration, thus making them more and more shareholder-managers (and not employee-managers).

class does not prohibit all antagonistic reconfigurations. It is still possible to set history on the march again, or more accurately, to set in motion a possible history of transcending capitalism – but an open-ended history, not yet written and without any teleological guarantees. The driving antagonism of such a history cannot be simply that of 'capital and labour', although its task would be to overturn capital (but capital as a reified social relation). What could then be the structuring principle of this new antagonism? The answer is, again, the affects – more precisely, the clash between the joyful who want nothing changed, and who want more of the same, and the discontented who want something else.

Discontent then is the affective historical force that is capable of bifurcating the course of events. Like social life as a whole, of which it is simply the temporal unfolding, history runs on affects. But 'bifurcatory' history runs specifically on angry affects. The multitude that is capable of gathering enough power to bring about great reversals is the multitude of malcontents. Nothing prevents us from continuing to talk about class, contrarily to the claims of a certain sociology eager to shed its Marxism to be more in tune with the liberal mood of the time. Classes very much continue to exist because, by virtue of the very fact that experiences are strongly determined by an individual's social situation, a community or proximity of experiences determines a community or proximity of ways of feeling, forming opinions and desiring. But this definition of class does not possess the simplicity of the initial bipolar scheme, since belonging to the 'employee-class' (the class of 'labour') is no longer in itself as strongly predetermining as it used to be; crucially, it no longer has the homogeneity that enabled it (at times) to act as a historical driving force. Nevertheless, this relative fragmentation of the class structure and the ensuing blurring of the social landscape in no way prevents re-homogenisations from taking place, but these must follow a different logic, notably, the affective logic of discontent. Therefore, the prospect of class war, not as a latent and stabilised tension but as an open confrontation, has not in the least disappeared. But it has changed its contents and dividing lines: it is an affective class war (or a war of affective classes). Contrary to what might be imagined, putting things this way is not merely a way of paying lip service to Marx in order to better dispose of him. Common affects do not fall from the sky; one must still ask what prior common affection produced them. In the present case it is rather on the side of capital that one must look, not so much capital as an antagonistic class – of which a solid core remains thoroughly identifiable, although its contours and periphery have become fuzzier – but capital as social relation, and ultimately as the very form of social life.

For the contemporary paradox of capitalism consists in that, at the very moment when it strives to increase the sophistication of its methods so as to develop a satisfied workforce, it mistreats employees at levels and intensities that have been unheard-of for decades. Becoming hateable while striving to make itself liked, capitalism spreads discontent and feeds 'the common passion by which a multitude could come together'.[40] There are evidently many slips between cup and lip, and the whole of political sociology comes to mind when we think of the very specific institutional and political conditions under which isolated instances of discontent succeed in coalescing, to acquire the consistency of a force of historical change.[41] But it is at least a fact that the increasingly violent tensions related to the valorisation of capital are spreading all the way up to the classes of those 'employees on the side of capital', raising the prospect of them switching sides. When the generalisation of capitalist mistreatment begins to touch the employees who

---

40   Paraphrasing *Political Treatise*, VI, 1.
41   See for example Michel Dobry, *Sociologie des crises politiques*, Presses de Sciences-Po, 1992.

until now tended to be the most committed, it effectively feeds a trend towards a 'Marxian' re-coincidence between their actual situation and their affective situation; namely, they revert to full and complete membership of the canonical employee-class. In sum, the growing discontent that emanates from the most dominated strata of the employee-class, to which it was supposed to remain confined, has the effect of producing a kind of 'reclarification' of the class situation and the restoration of the original landscape. It is this homogeneous and expanding class of malcontents that then threatens to turn against capitalism – and to set history on the march again.

COMMUNISM, DESIRE, AND SERVITUDE!

Were this class, reconstituted in a particular conjunction, to succeed in toppling the capitalist order and replacing it with new social forms of production such as the recommune, would that spell the end of the figure of the master-desire? Unfortunately, that is unlikely, for two reasons: first, because the pattern of a proposition made by one initiator to a community-to-be-constituted will very likely take its place; then, because the necessity of composing powers keeps raising the question of the relations under which this composition takes place – symmetrical or asymmetrical, flat or vertical (hierarchical) – and because, *in itself*, the division of labour distorts composition from the outset in the direction of hierarchical asymmetry. Yet the division (composition) of labour is our horizon, if only as an effect of ambition, that is, of a desire that dreams *big* (beyond the limits of its individual capacities). It is undoubtedly not by chance that Marx paid full attention to the division of labour, not only as an economist but also as a political thinker. One can deplore in this regard those overhasty readings of Marx that sought to situate the question of the capitalist relations of power in the exclusive orbit of the regime of ownership of the means of production, overlooking the division of labour despite the strongly structuring effects that Marx attributed to it in both *The German Ideology* and *Capital*.[42] To be sure, no one would deny that the private ownership of capital has effects. But these effects are asymmetrical; more accurately, one could say that a re-examination of private ownership is a necessary but not a sufficient condition. Did the full state ownership of the means of production in the USSR change in any way the social relations of production? Indeed, Lenin did not hesitate to recognise in nascent Fordism a model of industrial organisation. As for the experience of the Soviets, it did not even last a year. For as Marx explained, the division of labour itself *endogenously* secretes power [*pouvoir*], solely by virtue of reserving to some of its positions the distinctive tasks of coordination and the synthesis-totalisation of information, while leaving other producers with only a fragmentary view. Power is therefore continuously regenerated inside collective production out of these functional and informational asymmetries. At the very least, such an account should seriously dampen our enthusiasm for a transformation that would be limited to the regime of ownership. While it is clearly imperative to dismantle the private capitalist form of ownership, we cannot dispense with inventing 'the next episode'.

Contrary to what one may expect, Spinoza too was interested in the division of labour. Significantly, he devoted to this subject his first reflections on what holds people together and makes them establish communities – in Chapter 5 of the *Theological-Political Treatise*.[43] For Spinoza, the division of

---

42   Notably in Chapters 14 and 15 of Book I.

43   Benedictus de Spinoza, *Theological-Political Treatise*, trans. Michael Silverthorne, Cambridge University Press, 2007. We are indebted to Pierre-François Moreau for underlining that, in addition to Chapters 16 and 17 explicitly devoted to 'contract', Chapter 5 offers an outline of an alternative constitutional model of the state, which is in addition endogenous. See Pierre-François

labour is both what is best in people, a necessity of sorts that reminds them that 'to men, there is nothing more useful than men',[44] thus pushing them towards one another, and what is worst in people, since they always enter the compositions of powers unequally armed, an asymmetry that is at the root of all captures. Furthermore, they enter it unequally desiring. Even in those associations a priori based on the most equal rules, there is always someone who wants more than the others, who is more concerned by the goal of the association, more intensely interested in it, who wants its profits more – for there are always profits to be had. Not all activities fall inside the money economy, but not a single one stands outside the economy of joy. The conatus is a desiring force, and desire is constitutively interested in its object – another way of saying that it seeks joy. Taking many forms besides money, the profits of joy are the very *telos* of action, or else its price; they determine whether it is continued or abandoned. The pursuit of monetary profit is therefore only a special case of a general economy of joy, in which every action, whether individual or collective, is necessarily immersed and seeks its paths.

The constraints on collective action that result from this condition are especially strong when this action seeks extrinsic joys, that is, joys attached not to accomplishing the goal of the enterprise in itself – the enjoyment of the object as such – but to obtaining it *under the gaze of others*, and stronger still when the primary goal is to gain the approval of *public opinion* for an accomplishment; namely, when the enterprise falls into that particular economy of joy which is the economy of recognition. In contrast to the (non-capitalist) economy of intrinsic joy, with its non-adversarial enjoyment of the collectively produced

Moreau, 'Les deux genèses de l'État dans le *Traité théologico-politique*', in *Spinoza, État et religion*, ENS Éditions, 2005.

44 *Ethics*, IV, 18, Scholium.

object, the economy of extrinsic joy remains differential and competitive. Collective enterprises therefore have their cohesion forever threatened by desires of monopolistic appropriation aimed at obtaining extrinsic joys, namely, the joy of contemplating oneself as the cause of the joys of others. 'And since this [joy] is renewed as often as a man considers his virtues, *or* his power of acting, everyone is anxious to tell his own deeds, and show off his powers, both of body and of mind, and . . . men, for this reason, are a nuisance to one another.'[45] Taking Spinoza's words beyond the literal sense, we could clarify that the nuisance is not only the bragging itself, but also the unjustified individual capture of the (extrinsic) joyful profits of collective action, and the struggles that often follow. Moreover, nothing is easier than self-delusion about one's power, for example when I ascribe to myself the totality of a product to which other powers, joined to mine, have nevertheless contributed: 'the work is collective, but it's my work.' And capture is in essence *attributive* capture.

A hypothetical exit from capitalism and its economy of monetary joy would by no means do away with the perils of capture, which would remain fully operative in a non-monetary economy of recognition. Moreover, the formal correspondence between these two economies of joy is striking: in both cases one adds other powers to one's own in order to increase the effect produced and the extrinsic joyful benefit that accompanies it – and that can be captured. Those who enter the association desiring more intensely, who imagine better than others the profits of recognition of the collective work and want it more, those are the potential appropriators, the aspiring monopolisers of extrinsic joys. They are the new figure of the master-desire, reconstituted outside the formal structures of capture, namely, outside the structures of the various bossing

---

45   Ibid., III, 55, Scholium.

relations, and against a background of equal engagement – but equal only in appearance, for the intensities of desire were different. Thus, even outside the social relations that formally institute capture, the dynamics of passionate interests is sufficiently powerful to recreate that which the association wanted to avoid. And every association faces the permanent risk of having a member who offers 'to take matters in hand', a statement that should cause alarm to fellow members, for it must be read literally as a notice of pronation, namely, of an intention to monopolise and take everything for oneself, the intention of an appropriating desire that is bound to mutate quickly into a commanding desire.

Having begun this book with a Kantian parenthesis, the maxim that prohibits reducing people to the status of means, we could end in the same way and ask what, in these matters of capture and liberation, 'we are allowed to hope for'. It is a question for which we should want an unvarnished answer: every disappointment is proportional to the hopes that preceded it, and it would be an understatement to say that the idea of communism, or the idea of breaking with capitalism, was full of hope. It is also a way of not losing sight of that hard intellectual virtue of materialism that Althusser defined as 'no longer fooling oneself'.[46] Spinoza already gave his own version when he asked his readers to take people 'as they are' and not 'as they themselves would like them to be'.[47] The writer on politics who fails to take this precaution is condemned to produce nothing but 'a chimera, or [something that] might have been formed in Utopia, or in that golden age of the poets when, to be sure, there was least need for it'.[48] The meaning of this warning is as clear as can be: as much as capitalism, but in a totally different way,

---

46 Cited in Clément Rosset, *En ce temps-là. Notes sur Louis Althusser*, Minuit, 1992, p. 22.

47 *Political Treatise*, I, 1.

48 Ibid.

communism too must contend with desire and its passions, namely, with the 'force of the affects' responsible, not for the local oddities of voluntary servitude, but for the permanence of universal 'human servitude'.[49] Almost negatively, as its real condition of possibility seems so far away from us, it is again Spinoza who gives us perhaps the definition of true communism: passionate exploitation comes to an end when people know how to guide their common desires – and form enterprises, but communist ones – towards goals that are no longer subject to unilateral capture; namely, when they understand that the truly good is what one must wish for others to possess at the same time as oneself. This is for example the case with reason, that all must want the greatest possible number to possess, since 'insofar as men live according to the guidance of reason, they are most useful to man'.[50] But this redirection of desire and this understanding of things are precisely the goal of Spinoza's *Ethics*, and he does not hide that 'the way [is] very hard.'[51]

'A HUMAN LIFE'

This is in fact an understatement, since it assumes people are not in the grip of the passions, but guided by reason. *Ex ductu rationis*, people know that they must unrestrictedly want for others the joys they seek for themselves, and 'want nothing for themselves which they do not desire for other[s]'.[52] But this is indeed the highest formula of communism, resting on the generalised non-rivalry of the (true) goods, which can therefore be genuinely produced and enjoyed in common, namely, rid of the capturing efforts of individual desires that the

---

49   The origin of the name of the fourth book of the *Ethics*.
50   *Ethics*, IV, 37, Demonstration 1.
51   Ibid., V, 42, Scholium.
52   Ibid., IV, 18, Scholium.

passionate life otherwise keeps recreating. Only non-rivalry really saves us from the figure of the master-desire. But it requires people living lives guided by reason, and this is not a minor presupposition. The overthrow of capitalism is not in itself enough to satisfy it. For if capitalism's social structures take capture to the extreme, they largely draw on the resources of the passionate life that pre-existed it – and that will survive it. Seeing how it is generated endogenously in situations a priori designed to avoid it, one could almost come to the conclusion that the *formal structure of capture* must have something like its own conatus. One might say less allusively that it is a very strong attractor of the passionate life, as demonstrated by those extreme cases where it falls to those who have not even asked for it (like Pascal's castaway, made king by the inhabitants of the island where his ship ran aground).[53] That is why true communism does not come about *immediately* just because capitalism has been (hypothetically) defeated, at least if by communism we mean the final emancipation from the figure of the master-desire.

Thus, 'the free development of each, the condition for the free development of all' is less simple an affair than Marx and Engels suggested in the *Manifesto*. The best means of saving the idea of liberation is by breaking with the idea of the final 'big night' of liberation, the apocalyptic showdown followed by the sudden and miraculous irruption of a totally different kind of human and social relations. But while human and social relations cannot become *totally* different from one day to the next, they can become different, even significantly so. For the radical disjunction between life guided by reason and life in the grip of the passions entails neither that everything pertaining to the former amounts to the same, nor that on the 'bad' side of the divide everything

---

53   Pascal, 'First Discourse'.

is undifferentiated. The servitude inherent in the passionate condition – it is indeed servitude since it is hetero-determination, attachment to external causes and things – is not in contradiction with the diversity of institutional arrangements that govern the flow of human passions, which are always already social passions for that very reason. And not all arrangements are equal. Shaped in diverse ways by different structures and institutions, passions interacting and entering in composition with one another determine strikingly different possibilities of power [*puissance*], desire and joy. A Commonwealth whose institutional arrangements only move subjects to function through fear, and where 'peace depends on the sluggishness of its subjects, that are led about like sheep, to learn but slavery, may more properly be called a solitude than a commonwealth'.[54] The yoke of sad affects is no less a yoke than that of joyful affects, but it is, well, sad – which is quite a difference. Nor is it the same form of life. For subjects who are led by fear are riveted, indi-vidually and collectively, to the lowest level of power, and the contrast between a multitude led by hope more than by fear and a multitude primarily subdued by fear is immediately recognisable: 'the former aims at making use of life, the latter but at escaping death.'[55] This is then the ground for drawing up a hierarchy of the different regimes of the collective passionate life: not by loosening passions' servitude, but according to the difference in how the interplay of their institutional expressions empowers individuals and allows them to rejoice. 'When, then, we call that dominion best, where men pass their lives in unity, I understand a human life, defined not by mere circulation of the blood, and other

---

54   *Political Treatise*, V, 4. I take the liberty here of changing the [French] translation of Charles Ramond by restituting Charles Appuhn's 'solitude' in place of 'desert'.

55   Ibid., V, 6.

qualities common to all animals, but above all by reason, the true excellence and life of the mind.'[56]

The end of the social relations of capitalism does not mean the end of our passionate servitude. It does not by itself free us from the disorderly violence of desire and the efforts of power. It is perhaps on this precise point that the Spinozist realism of the passions is most useful to the Marxian utopia: as a sobering-up. The extinction of politics by the final dissolution of classes and the conflict between them, transcending all antagonisms by the victory of the working class, that non-class without any class interest, are post-political phantasmagoria, perhaps Marx's deepest anthropological error,[57] which consists in dreaming of a final eradication of violence – when there is no horizon except the search for the least destructive ways of organising it. Spinoza makes the point that if all people were wise, namely, led by reason, they would need neither laws nor political institutions. But wise is precisely what they are not, which is why they have no choice but to take into consideration the passionate move-ments of the conatus, which, of itself, 'is not opposed to strifes, hatred, anger, treachery, or, in general, anything that appetite suggests.'[58] Neither the recommune nor transcending capital-ism liberates us from this element of violence, nor does it exempt us from reinventing institutional regulations for it. That is why, if we use the word to mean radical liberation, we must recognise that communism is a long patience, a continuous effort, and perhaps only, to speak again like Kant, a regulative idea. Let us not even mention, in keeping with the illusions of subjectivity, a liberation in the sense of the sovereignty of a perfectly autonomous ego. Passionate exo-determination is our irremissible condition. Let us also not dream of the final

---

56 Ibid., V, 5.

57 Karl Marx, *Critique of Hegel's Philosophy of Right*, Aristeus Books, 2012, p. 12.

58 *Political Treatise*, II, 8.

abolition of relations of dependence. It is impossible for the interest of one to never have to pass through another, and that no effect of domination would follow: love-interests, whether in erotic form or that of the desire for recognition, pass by their very nature through chosen others, individual or collective. These desires-interests, the very expression of the amorous logic of the conatus and of its passionate servitude, imperiously and at times violently cut a path for themselves, and neither transformations in the forms of ownership nor the generalisation of associative relations could fully disarm them. If true communism consists in living *ex ductu rationis*, it is better to recognise that it is a horizon and forego early the illusions of the radiant society.

But to forego the *telos* is not to forego every progress that can take place in its direction. Any reconfiguration of the regime of passions that has the effect of pushing the figure of capture a little further away is worthwhile. What arrangements of our collective life maximise the effectuations of our powers of acting and our powers of thinking? This is exactly the question posed by the *Political Treatise*, which is in this sense the first realist *manifesto*, not of the communist party, but of communist life, for another name for the communist life could be radical democracy. This question runs through the whole of the *Treatise*, most often in what is left unsaid, or if one prefers, implicitly. Yet it is unmistakably present since Spinoza always leads the facts of power [*pouvoir*], namely, the facts of capture, back to the immanent power [*puissance*] of the multitude. There is no *potestas* that does not emanate from *potentia* (*multitudinis*)[59] – but in the form of hijacking and to the advantage of the most powerful of master-desires, the desire of the

---

59   Matheron, *Individu et communauté*; Antonio Negri, *Savage Anomaly: The Power of Spinoza's Metaphysics and Politics*, University of Minnesota Press, 1999.

sovereign. However, of all these regimes, only democracy organises the reunion of the multitude with its own power.[60] 'I pass, at length, to the third and perfectly absolute dominion, which we call democracy.'[61] Thus begins the eleventh chapter of the *Political Treatise*, an unfinished chapter that is left for us as a sort of opening, at once opaque and vertiginous: *omino absolutum imperium*. Spinoza is not in the habit of using words carelessly, and we sense already that the promise of the 'perfectly absolute dominion' is none other than that of the multitude regaining its sovereignty. The unfinished *Treatise* leaves us the task of discovering the conditions and inventing the ways of this second coming of sovereignty, in other words, to rediscover, in order to finally give it residence in time, that 'original' flash-moment, fictional of course, but conceptually meaningful, when the multitude manifested its sovereign power – before being immediately dispossessed by the operation of all the mechanisms of capture and the constitution of the vertical structures of power. Below the primary master-desire, that of the sovereign, other master-desires have blossomed, reproducing the sovereign's capturing gesture, favoured by the entirety of social structures, to say nothing of the spontaneous dynamics of the passionate life. It is evidently progress that, mediated by the effects of epithumogenic efforts, the iron fists of brute coercion and of the various bossing enslavements have mutated into joyful subjections. But it is a second-order progress within sameness – the sameness of the master-desire and of capture,

---

60 It may seem incoherent to bring back here, after having excluded it above, the scheme of the de-separation of a body and its power. But here we are dealing with the social body, and de-separation is seen from the point of view of *the parts* in so far as they form an idea about the whole that includes them. Even though, as all bodies, the social body never does anything except what it can, no more and no less, there remains a sense in which people consider that their collective acting and its products have fallen out of their control – and want to regain a certain level of mastery.

61 *Political Treatise*, XI, 1.

which is also the sameness of passionate exploitation. For, despite all the joyful attire that it strives to don for the purpose of maximising its own effectiveness, passionate exploitation is by nature the fixation of the enlistees' power of acting onto the goals and intermediate objectives assigned it by the master-desire, and therefore is a relative disempowerment. To liberate individuals from the custody, sad or joyful, of the master-desire, to the extent possible and even if final liberation is only a horizon, is not only to do away with the asymmetries of the capture and their retinue of dominations, but also to reopen the spectrum of possibilities for the effectuations of their power.

Since we are doomed to exo-determination, there is no possibility of being outside alienation. But it does not follow that all forms of alienation are equal. Some present individuals with wider latitudes for desiring and enjoying, releasing them from the fixed ideas of the master-desires that other forms compel them to live under. The common life is not a choice that people are free to reject. The endogenous forces of their passionate lives lead them to it necessarily, beginning with the requisites for reproducing their material lives.[62] But the relations that govern the organisation of this common life are neither written in advance nor given for all eternity, and it is thus permitted to prefer some over others. Their invention and production inside the real of history is the unpredictable effect of the dynamics of collective affective life – also known as politics. If the idea has meaning, progress can only be the enrichment of life in joyful affects, and particularly in those that widen the field of possibilities for the effectuations of our power and lead them to direct themselves towards 'the real good', by which 'I understand a human life'.

---

62 *Ethics*, IV, 37, Scholia 1 and 2; *Theological-Political Treatise*, V, 7; *Political Treatise*, II, 15.

Bibliography

Aglietta, Michel and André Orléan, *La violence de la monnaie*, PUF, 1982.
———. (eds), *La monnaie souveraine*, Odile Jacob, 1998.
———. (eds) *La monnaie entre violence et confiance*, Odile Jacob, 2002.
Alis, David, "'Travail émotionnel, dissonance émotionnelle et contrefaçon de l'intimité'. Vingt-cinq ans après la publication de *Managed Heart* d'Arlie R. Hochschild', in Isabelle Berrebi-Hoffmann, *Politiques de l'intime. Des utopies sociales d'hier aux mondes du travail d'aujourd'hui*, La Découverte, 2009.
Artous, Antoine, *Travail et émancipation sociale. Marx et le travail*, Éditions Syllepse, 2003.
Balibar, Étienne, *Spinoza and Politics*, Verso, 2008.
Baranski, Laurence, *Le manager éclairé, pilote du changement*, Éditions d'Organisation, 2001.
Barthes, Roland, *Camera Lucida: Reflections on Photography*, Hill and Wang, 1981, reprint 2010.
Bidet, Jacques and Gérard Duménil, *Altermarxisme. Un autre marxisme pour un autre monde*, PUF, 2007.
Boltanski, Luc and Eve Chiapello, *The New Spirit of Capitalism*, Verso, 2007.
Bourdieu, Pierre, *Choses dites*, Minuit, 1987.
Bove, Laurent, *La stratégie du conatus. Affirmation et résistance chez Spinoza*, Vrin, 1996.
—, '*Éthique*, partie III', in Moreau, Pierre-François and Charles Ramond (eds), *Lectures de Spinoza*, Ellipses, 2006.
Boyer, Robert, *Regulation Theory: The State of the Art*, Routledge, 2002.
Caillat, Gérald and Pierre Legendre, *Dominus Mundi. L'empire du management*, DVD, Idéale Audience, ARTE France.
Camus, Albert, *Caligula and Other Plays*, trans. Justin O'Brien, Vintage, 1962.
Cette, Gilbert, Jacques Delpla and Arnaud Sylvain, *Le partage des fruits de la croissance en France*, Rapport du CAE n° 85, La Documentation Française, 2009.
Citton, Yves, *Mythocratie. Storytelling et imaginaire de gauche*, Éditions Amsterdam, 2010.
Coutrot, Thomas, *L'entreprise néolibérale, nouvelle utopie capitaliste?*, La Découverte, 1998.
Dardot, Pierre and Christian Laval, *La nouvelle raison du monde. Essai sur la société néolibérale*, La Découverte, 2009. In English translation, *The New Way of the World: On Neoliberal Society*, trans. Gregory Elliott, Verso, 2014.
Deleuze, Gilles, *Proust and Signs*, University of Minnesota Press, 2004.
Delumeau, Jean, *L'aveu et le pardon*, Fayard, 1990.
Damasio, Antonio, *L'Erreur de Descartes*, Odile Jacob, 1995.
Denord, François and Antoine Schwartz, *L'Europe sociale n'aura pas lieu*, Éditions Raisons d'agir, 2009.
Dobry, Michel, *Sociologie des crises politiques*, Presses de Sciences-Po, 1992.
Dujarier, Marie-Anne, *L'idéal au travail*, PUF, 2006.

Duménil, Gérard and Dominique Lévy, *Économie marxiste du capitalisme*, La Découverte, 2003.

Durand, Jean-Pierre and Marie-Christine Le Floch (eds), *La question du consentement au travail. De la servitude volontaire à l'implication contrainte*, L'Harmattan, 2006.

Durkheim, Émile, *Sociology and Philosophy*, Routledge, 2010.

Elias, Norbert, *The Civilizing Process: Sociogenetic and Psychogenetic Investigations*, Blackwell, 2000.

Falafil, 'Quel paradigme du don ? En clé d'intérêt ou en clé de don ? Réponse à Frédéric Lordon', in 'De l'anti-utilitarisme. Anniversaire, bilan et controverses', *Revue du MAUSS semestrielle* 27 (2006).

Fischbach, Franck, *Sans objet. Capitalisme, subjectivité, aliénation*, Vrin, 2009.

Foucault, Michel, 'The Subject and Power', in Hubert L. Dreyfus and Paul Rabinow, *Michel Foucault: Beyond Structuralism and Hermeneutics*, Harvester Press, 1982.

Gasparini, William, 'Dispositif managérial et dispositions sociales au consentement. L'exemple du travail de vente d'articles de sport', in Durand and Le Floch (eds), *La question du consentement au travail*.

Gauléjac, Vincent de, *La société malade de la gestion*, Seuil, 2004.

Gillot, Pascale, *L'esprit, figures classiques et contemporaines*, CNRS Éditions, 2007.

Guilhaume, Geneviève, *L'ère du coaching. Critique d'une violence euphémisée*, Syllepse, 2009.

Hayek, Friedrich A. 'The Persistence of Constructivism in Current Thought', in *Law, Legislation and Liberty*, Routledge, 2012.

Johnson, Simon, 'The Quiet Coup', *The Atlantic*, thetlantic.com.doc/200905/imfadvice, 2009.

Kant, Immanuel, *Grounding of Metaphysics of Morals*, 3rd ed., trans. James W. Ellington, Hackett, 1993.

La Boétie, Étienne de, *The Discourse of Voluntary Servitude*, Hackett, 2012.

Levi, Primo, *Survival at Auschwitz*, Touchstone, 1995.

Limann, Teodor, *Morts de peur. La vie de bureau*, Les empêcheurs de penser en rond, 2007.

Lordon, Frédéric, *La politique du capital*, Odile Jacob, 2002

———. *La crise de trop. Reconstruction d'un monde failli*, Fayard, 2009.

———. 'Le don tel qu'il est et non qu'on voudrait qu'il fût', in 'De l'anti-utilitarisme', *Revue du MAUSS semestrielle* 27 (2006).

———. 'L'empire des institutions', *Revue de la Régulation* 7 (2010), regulation. revues.org.

———. 'Homo passionalis æconomicus', *Actes de la Recherche en Sciences Sociales*, conference paper given at 'Economie et fabrique de la subjectivité', Association française de psychiatrie, Paris, 2010.

———. *L'intérêt souverain. Essai d'anthropologie économique spinoziste*, La Découverte, 2006.

———. and André Orléan, 'Genèse de l'État et genèse de la monnaie: le modèle de la *potentia multitudinis*', in Citton, Y. and F. Lordon, *Spinoza et les sciences sociales. De la puissance de la multitude à l'économie des affects*, Éditions Amsterdam, 2008.

———. *Et la vertu sauvera le monde. Après la crise financière, le salut par 'L'éthique'?*, Raisons d'Agir, 2003.

———. 'La puissance des institutions', *Revue du MAUSS permanente* (April 2010), journaldumauss.net.

———. 'La légitimité n'existe pas. Éléments pour une théorie des institutions', *Cahiers d'Économie Politique* 53 (2007).

Maître, Jacques, *L'autobiographie d'un paranoïaque*, Anthropos, 1994.

Marx, Karl, *Capital, Volume 1: A Critique of Political Economy*, Penguin, reprint 1992.

———. *Critique of Hegel's Philosophy of Right*, Aristeus Books, 2012.

———. and Friedrich Engels, 'The German Ideology', in *The German Ideology including Theses on Feuerbach*, Prometheus Books, 1998.

Matheron, Alexandre, *Individu et communauté chez Spinoza*, Minuit, 1988.

Menger, Pierre-Michel, *Portrait de l'artiste en travailleur. Métamorphoses du capitalisme*, Seuil, 2006.

Moreau, Pierre-François, 'Les deux genèses de l'État dans le *Traité théologico-politique*', in *Spinoza, État et religion*, ENS Éditions, 2005.

Nagy, Piroska, *Le don des larmes au Moyen-Âge*, Albin Michel, 2000.

Negri, Antonio, *Savage Anomaly: The Power of Spinoza's Metaphysics and Politics*, University of Minnesota Press, 1999.

Orléan, André, 'L'individu, le marché et l'opinion: réflexions sur le capitalisme financier', *Esprit* (November 2000).

Ould-Ahmed, Pepita, 'Monnaie des anthropologues, argent des économistes: à chacun le sien?' in E. Baumann, L. Bazin, P. Ould-Ahmed, P. Phélinas, M. Selim, R. Sobel (eds), *L'argent des anthropologues, la monnaie des économistes*, L'Harmattan, 2008.

Pascal, Blaise, *Pensées and Other Writings*, trans. Honor Levi, Oxford University Press, 2008.

———. 'Three Discourses on the Condition of the Great', trans. Samuel Webb, marxists.org/reference/archive/pascal/1630.

Perret, Gilles, *Ma mondialisation*, DVD, Les Films du Paradoxe, 2006.

Plato, *Gorgias*, trans. Donald Zeyl, Hackett, 1986.

Poster, Winifred, 'Who's on the Line? Indian Call Center Agents Pose as Americans for US-Outsourced Firms', *Industrial Relations* 46, n° 2 (2007).

Postone, Moishe, *Time, Labor, and Social Domination: A Reinterpretation of Marx's Critical Theory*, Cambridge University Press, 1996.

Prévieux, Julien, *Lettres de non-motivation*, Archon, 2000.

Rancière, Jacques, *Disagreement: Politics and Philosophy*, University of Minnesota Press, 2004.

———. *The Nights of Labor: The Workers' Dream in Nineteenth-Century France*, trans. John Drury, Temple University Press, 1989.

Rosset, Clément, *En ce temps-là. Notes sur Louis Althusser*, Minuit, 1992.

Rouaud, Christian, *Les Lip. L'imagination au pouvoir*, DVD, Les Films du Paradoxe, 2007.

Ruffin, François, *La guerre des classes*, Fayard, 2008.

Sévérac, Pascal, 'Le devenir actif du corps affectif', *Astérion* 3 (September 2005), asterion.revues.org.

———. *Le devenir actif chez Spinoza*, Honoré Champion, 2005.

Spinoza, Benedict de, *Ethics*, in *A Spinoza Reader, The Ethics and Other Works*, trans. Edwin Curley, Princeton University Press, 1994.

———. *On the Improvement of the Understanding, the Ethics, Correspondence*, trans. R. H. M. Elwes, Dover 1995.

——. *The Letters*, trans. Samuel Shirley, Hackett, 1995.

——. *Political Treatise*, trans. A. H. Gosset, G. Bell & Son, 1883. HTML version, constitution.org.

——. *Theological-Political Treatise*, trans. Michael Silverthorne, Cambridge University Press, 2007.

Théret, Bruno, 'La monnaie au prisme de ses crises d'hier et d'aujourd'hui', in B. Théret (ed.), *La monnaie dévoilée par ses crises*, Éditions de l'EHESS, 2007.

Tietmeyer, Hans, *Économie sociale de marché et stabilité monétaire*, Economica, 1999.

Viallet, Jean-Robert, *La mise à mort du travail*, DVD, Yami2 Productions, 2009.

Vinciguerra, Lorenzo, *Spinoza et le signe. Genèse de l'imagination*, Vrin, 2005.

Zourabichvili, François, *Spinoza, une physique de la pensée*, PUF, 2002.

Index